Nelson Handwriting

NELSON

HANDWRITING

Infant Teacher's Manual

ALEXANDER INGLIS B.Sc., Dip. Ed., F.E.I.S.
and ELIZABETH CONNELL

Consultant
Dr DOUGLAS M. McINTOSH M.A., B.Sc., Ph. Dr.,
F.E.I.S., F.R.S.E., O.B.E.

Thomas Nelson and Sons Ltd
Nelson House Mayfield Road Walton-on-Thames Surrey KT12 5PL
PO Box 18123 Nairobi Kenya
Watson Estate Block A 13 Floor
Watson Road Causeway Bay Hong Kong
116-D JTC Factory Building Lorong 3 Geylang Square Singapore 14

Thomas Nelson Australia Pty Ltd
19–39 Jeffcott Street West Melbourne Victoria 3003

Nelson Canada Ltd
81 Curlew Drive Don Mills Ontario M3A 2R1

Thomas Nelson (Nigeria)Ltd
8 Ilupeju Bypass PMB 21303 Ikeja Lagos

© Thomas Nelson and Sons Limited 1964

Reprinted 1978, 1979, 1980

ISBN 0 17 414003 7
NCN 0089 11 7

Printed in Hong Kong

Contents

Contents

PART ONE

GENERAL THEORY

PART ONE

GENERAL THEORY

Introduction

The aim of these books on handwriting is to show how children may be taught to acquire from an early age a fluent, legible style of handwriting, which will not only serve their everyday needs in school, but will also meet the demands of later life for speedy and graceful writing.

Handwriting is essentially a tool subject. Its prime function is to meet the needs of all other subjects. Its essential qualities are legibility and fluency ; they are of equal importance and only when they are taught together does writing stay taught.

Handwriting is also the most universal of all crafts and must be judged by aesthetic as well as by utilitarian standards.

STYLE

It would be wrong to expect every child to write in an identical style. The letters illustrated in the schemes and work books are the proto-types from which each child's individual style should develop and derive.

The simple letter forms learned in the infant room are developed continuously, with only minor modifications, throughout the infant and primary stages. They are easy to teach and are easily learned by children whatever their level of ability, and if taught by the methods suggested do not readily become illegible even when written at considerable speed. When written with a square-edged pen in the later primary stages, an extremely pleasing, modern, italic hand is produced.

At the infant stage an unjoined script is advocated. At the

primary stages no attempt is made to join all letters in words. Ligatures are used only where they come easily and naturally and are an aid to the fluency and rhythm of writing.

METHOD

The teaching of handwriting is largely the teaching of movements. The skilled writer produces these movements speedily, rhythmically, and almost wholly automatically. If her efforts are to be fully effective, the teacher must have a thorough knowledge of the mechanics of handwriting and be familiar with the psychological and pedagogical principles applicable to the teaching and learning of these movements. The methods detailed in this scheme are based on recent research and classroom experience.

Frequent but brief periods of intensive, systematic instruction and practice in writing are necessary if the pupil's skill is to be fully developed.

Handwriting is, however, not merely a mechanical skill. It is a form of communication and self-expression, and the meaning of what is written must not be separated in the mind of the child from the act of writing. Skill in writing, especially in the earliest stages, is, therefore, developed largely through the writing of meaningful material and purposeful activities that will interest the child and elicit his co-operation and effort.

I

Summary of Work
in the Infant Classes

The guiding principle, not merely at the beginning of learning to write but at all stages of instruction, must be that the child is ready physically, emotionally and mentally to proceed to each new step. The desire to write, the reason for and purpose of writing, the success likely to be achieved, the child's perceptual, manipulative and reading ability are all factors of the state of readiness for writing. Premature formal instruction is certain to be not merely inefficient but may inhibit the future development of the skill.

There must, therefore, be an initial preparatory period devoted to observation and assessment of each child and to activities and instruction designed to promote readiness for writing.

LEARNING TO WRITE IS LEARNING
TO MAKE MOVEMENTS

Writing is a complex motor habit which develops slowly with maturation, training and practice. Learning to write is essentially learning to make movements. It involves the acquisition of unified motor habits for each letter and numeral, and eventually for combinations of letters. Letter forms are therefore to be learned not merely as visual forms or shapes to be recognised, named and drawn, but as *patterns of movement* to be performed rhythmically and smoothly, in one continuous movement where structure permits, and at a speed in keeping with the pupil's stage of neuromuscular development. The child must strive to write fluently at all stages of instruction, for the habit of fluent, legible writing can be established only if from the beginning letters and words are written freely and

3

rhythmically at a reasonable speed. Perfection of letter forms must not be sought during the infant stage at the expense of fluency. Improvement in the form of the letters written comes later.

THE MECHANICS OF HANDWRITING

Since the writing process is largely a mechanical operation, the mechanics of writing must receive adequate attention if optimum results are to be obtained. Much of the difficulty in teaching children to write well undoubtedly lies in the failure to realise that, although it is relatively easy to learn to write after a manner irrespective of the methods employed, it is virtually impossible to write fluently and well unless the writing mechanism is satisfactory.

Unless adequate attention is paid to correct posture, the correct method of holding and moving the writing instrument, to muscular relaxation and to the physical conditions in the classroom, the task of both teacher and pupil will be rendered unnecessarily difficult. Training must begin in the infant room so that pupils gradually acquire the writing habits essential to the production of fluent, legible and graceful writing at all stages of instruction.

It follows from the principles outlined in this and in the preceding section that *how* writing is produced is in every way as important as *what* is produced.

LETTER FORMS AND STYLE

The letter forms illustrated and used throughout the scheme were chosen only after much experimentation and discussion by experienced teachers. The letters illustrated are the basic skeletal forms from which the pupil's own personal style of writing will develop. The bodies of the letters *a, b, c, d, g, o, p* and *q* are oval or elliptical since this is the movement which can be made most naturally and easily by any of the modern writing instruments. This oval form of letter lacks none of the advantages claimed for the round script based on geometrical construction which has been in common use. It will be found that it is more easily produced than the round form and to this extent the task of both teacher and pupil is eased. It has

4

the further advantage that the majority of the letters can be taught as single continuous rhythmic movements, and as the same letter forms are used in primary classes, continuity of style and instruction is ensured.

By the end of two years in the infant room pupils should have learned to write all letters and numerals fluently and well even with the eyes closed. The unjoined script which they use for written work should by this stage be produced with such ease and fluency and with such little conscious attention to the form of letters and the mechanics of writing that undivided attention may be devoted to the content of the written matter.

CHILD-CENTRED INSTRUCTION

As the child proceeds from the first satisfying experience of writing his own name to the stage of writing original stories in a fluent and graceful hand, the teacher must constantly try to ensure that practice is meaningful and satisfying. This can only be so if writing is presented to the child in the terms of his own purposes and experiences and if he is so ready to proceed to every new step that reasonable success in the task is assured. Since the rate of progress and the standard of achievement for individual children at any given stage varies widely, writing must be taught in terms of individual differences and assessed as a product of the stage of maturation and development of the child. The left-handed child and the handicapped child must receive the special instruction and help they require. At all times the teacher must try to ensure that a desirable attitude to the skill of writing is cultivated.

WRITING LESSONS AND SCHEMES OF WORK

It is now commonly accepted that instruction in writing should begin with the writing of whole words, phrases or sentences rather than with letters or elements of letters.*

* *The Teaching of Handwriting*, by W. S. Gray, p. 193, *U.N.E.S.C.O. Monograph on Fundamental Education*. Evans Bros. Ltd.

The whole word has a meaning for the child and it is the meaning that gives purpose to writing. And so in the earliest stages the child is stimulated to draw words he knows when he sees them displayed on the blackboard or on cards in the classroom. Early instruction in handwriting should therefore be integrated with the teaching of reading and be part of many of the ordinary classroom activities. Writing then becomes interesting, satisfying and purposeful, and the conditions essential to ready learning are satisfied. The teacher will have many opportunities during these writing periods for giving help, for observing and correcting faulty techniques and for determining what new instruction is required.

Such instruction by itself is obviously inadequate as it is not sufficiently systematic and thorough, and not enough opportunities are afforded for attention to the basic writing techniques and for intensive practice of specific handwriting movements. This scheme is based on the assumption that after the required degree of readiness is reached, there must be, in addition to and concurrent with much informal practice, brief but frequent periods of systematic formal instruction and practice.

2

The Preparatory Period

Since children differ in their social background and in their physical, emotional and mental endowment and development, it is not surprising that they also differ widely in their readiness to receive instruction when they first enter school. Instruction in writing must be suited to the needs of the individual ; so the teacher must first observe and assess the capabilities and stage of development of each child and provide instruction and experiences which will assist him to reach the stage at which he will profit from formal instruction. Premature formal instruction may cause anxiety, failure to relax, retardation of neuromuscular development, and result in unnecessarily low standards of work at all future stages.

"Readiness for writing" means not merely the attainment of the necessary degree of physical development and manipulative skill to enable a child to write ; mental, emotional and social readiness are of equal importance.

PHYSICAL READINESS

The visual, muscular and nervous systems of young children are only partially developed. Children are unable to make the fine, precise movements of the hands and fingers required in mature writing and tire easily because they co-ordinate imperfectly. Up to the age of eight they tend to be far-sighted but under unfavourable conditions may become permanently near-sighted.

Early writing activities are in the main a continuation of the child's pre-school play selected with a view to developing muscular control and co-ordination of hand and eye. Directed play activities for the development of the larger muscles of the body and arms precede exercises for the development of the finer muscles of the hand and fingers. Exercises to develop sensory discrimination,

7

muscular and visual co-ordination, informal practice in writing, drawing and painting — all play a part at this stage in preparing the child physically for formal instruction.

MENTAL READINESS

A child is not ready to learn to write until he has reached the stage of being able to perceive minor differences in the form of letters, for he cannot be expected to reproduce what he cannot perceive. When he has learned to read, even to a limited degree, the teacher may be assured that the first writing lessons can be purposeful and meaningful to him.

READINESS AND MOTIVATION

Only when a child recognises the value and purpose of a task is he likely to tackle it eagerly and strive to achieve success. Fortunately the majority of young children are anxious to learn to write, and probably have attempted to do so long before they entered school. The teacher must not only stimulate the few who may have failed to reach this stage, but ensure that all maintain their first eagerness and delight in learning to write.

READINESS AND SUCCESS

A child will only persevere cheerfully and willingly with the tasks set when he continues to experience reasonable success. Continued inability to perform the task will result in either anxiety or apathy and unwillingness to apply himself with sufficient confidence and enthusiasm to fresh tasks.

A guiding principle at all stages of instruction must be that the child is so ready to proceed to every new step that success, if not assured, is reasonably to be expected.

Since individual pupils in a class vary in ability and attainment, it follows that much individual instruction is essential. The teacher must give assistance and encouragement whenever necessary, prepare the child for each new step and suit the nature and magnitude of each new task to the child's degree of readiness.

No formal lessons in writing should be given during the preparatory period. The teacher should not, however, neglect to make use of incidental opportunities for giving hints and help in acquiring correct techniques and helping pupils to make letters by the correct sequence of movements. Opportunities will arise for showing how to hold a pencil or brush lightly and in a reasonably correct manner, and how to stand at a blackboard or sit at a desk so that free writing movements are possible.

Much of the informal writing at this stage will be part of the activities associated with the initial stages in the teaching of reading. Pupils will attempt to draw letters and words met with during such lessons and should be encouraged to do so. They should also be given many opportunities for scribbling, drawing, painting, using tactile letters, rhythmic pattern-making to music or counting, and forming patterns or figures embodying movements to be met in making letters.

Stress is to be placed on the rhythm of production and the feel of the movement during writing at this stage.

During these early writing activities, the teacher must determine the degree of left-handedness of individual pupils and decide which hand they are to use when writing. (*see page* 30)

(*see page* 30)

DURATION OF THE PREPARATORY PERIOD

The time to be spent on any of the above-mentioned aspects of readiness will vary with individual children. A few will be quite ready when they first enter school ; some will not have reached this stage by the end of the first year. The guiding principle must be that the length of time for each child must be sufficient to prepare him for the first formal lessons. In Part Two of this book, a preparatory period of three months has been suggested.

3

Basic Principles, Techniques and Methods

(a) Teaching Letters and Numerals

When an infant copies an unfamiliar letter from the blackboard or a card, he is almost entirely dependent upon the visual control of the movement of the writing instrument. If the pencil is moved over the paper under the careful guidance of the eye and the writing of the character involves acts of attention to the successive lines and curves by which it is formed, the writing movements are likely to be hesitant and faltering.

When an older pupil or adult writes, the point of the pencil moves too quickly for the eye to follow, and far too quickly for the eyes to exercise control over the movements it makes. The shape of a character which is being written is determined mainly by the neuromuscular organisation of the writer. The movements are controlled and directed by the motor centres and there is little or no conscious attention to the visual form. It is only after a unified motor habit has been established for a character that it can be written at speed with ease and confidence.

Such unified motor habits which will result in the spontaneous production of the written form of a letter can be developed by prolonged practice in copying the shape of the character. The whole process of learning to write can, however, be more satisfactorily accomplished if letters are taught as patterns of movements to be acquired, and if the methods and apparatus used provide the kinaesthetic sensations which establish the required neuromuscular patterns.

Below are listed methods and activities which have been found efficacious in teaching letter forms as patterns of movement. No hard and fast order can be given for their use for they are in a measure complementary. Each method has its advantages and difficulties so that a pupil who fails with one method may succeed with another. The variety of approach and apparatus will help to sustain interest and facilitate the division of the class at a later stage into groups, each with a different writing activity. The teacher will also find that the activities described can be modified or varied to suit individual differences in ability and motor-muscular development.

SHAPE AND CONSTRUCTION

The first step must be the description of the starting point for the letter and the succession of movements by which it is made.

The teacher will trace with her finger over a large drawing of the letter on the blackboard giving at the same time a running commentary on the movements she is making, e.g. letter *c*

' Start here—up—over—round—down—round—up.'

While the teacher is tracing over the letter on the board the pupils should follow the movements by drawing in the air with a finger pointing to the blackboard model. The whole procedure should be repeated several times.

The teacher should then face the class and draw (in reverse) the letter in the air with the pupils following her movements with full arm movements. If this process is repeated several times the teacher will have an opportunity of noting pupils who have failed to perceive the form of the character.

The letter drawn on the blackboard or illustrated on cards must be the basic elementary form of the letter from which all possible future minor variations of form will derive. It must be drawn by the teacher in exactly the same way as the pupils will be expected to write it.

As soon as pupils have learned the starting point for a letter and the movements by which it is to be made they should be introduced to tactile letters from which the desired kinaesthetic sensations will be experienced as the child traces over the surface of the letter with his finger.

Such letters may consist of cut-outs made of wood, cardboard, plastic or metal; letters made of fine sandpaper, felt, velvet or card pasted on a solid surface; letters grooved in a solid surface, or a series of holes drilled in the shape of the letter in a solid surface. The letters should be at least 4 cm high. The starting point of each letter should preferably be indicated on the tactile letter by some such sign as a green arrow and the finishing point by a red bar or dot. After the child has traced the letter once or twice, further practice should be carried out by placing the finger at the starting point and then tracing the letter with the eyes closed.

Tactile letters should be used with a small group at a time to allow the teacher to make corrections at what is pedagogically the best time for correction—when the error is being made and not when it has become established by practice.

If lessons with the tactile letters are alternated with revision lessons on the method of writing given letters, the majority of pupils will soon be able to practise with the tactile letters without supervision. They can be used during group activity periods.

SAND-TRAYS

The method of drawing the letter in a sand-tray, at first with a finger and then with a stick scraping through the sand on to the bottom of the tray, has the advantage of leaving a record and of providing valuable kinaesthetic sensations.

A child who is particularly slow or is experiencing difficulty with a specific letter may be helped if the teacher guides his hand as his finger traces over a tactile letter or as he writes in the sand-tray.

Modelling a letter in plasticine does not help to establish directly the desired motor organisation, for the movements made in writing a letter are different from those made in modelling. The practice does, however, give the child a preliminary acquaintance with the form to be produced and gives it a meaning in physical terms. This method helps in the teaching of letters, such as *k*, which are not made with one continuous movement, especially if after the letter has been made correctly the child runs his finger over the surface of the letter with the correct series of movements.

TRACING WITH THE FINGER

The final step before using pencil or chalk is to trace the letter or numeral with the finger or with the blunt end of a pencil on the desk. Since this leaves no permanent record and it is difficult to observe if the letter is being made correctly, the teacher must watch carefully for accurate movements.

This method does, however, have very considerable advantages. No apparatus is required and it can therefore be very frequently used and for a few moments at any time. The letter can be traced many times if desired and so can play a very important part in establishing a motor habit, but since undesirable departures from the prototype letter form may become established but pass unnoticed by this method, it should be used with discretion.

This method can probably be used most advantageously either immediately before a letter or word is written on paper or blackboard, or interspersed with such writing.

WRITING WITH PENCIL, CHALK AND CRAYON

Pupils will have had many opportunities, during the preparatory period and during subsequent informal writing activities, of attempting to draw letters and words with various forms of writing instruments. The likelihood is that in these early stages they will draw them hesitatingly and inaccurately and possibly by incorrect movements.

The purpose of the methods and activities listed above is to show the pupil the starting point for each letter and the sequence of movements by which it is made, to give him a clear perception of the essential form of each letter and to provide practice rich in the kinaesthetic sensations which establish a neuromuscular pattern for each letter. If the child has had adequate instruction and practice with the methods and materials suggested he should be able to write the letters learned with complete confidence. He should, even from the start, be able to write them fairly speedily, rhythmically and with a surprising degree of accuracy. The aim from now on should be to give the child ample opportunity for writing the letters learned with increasing speed and rhythm. The child should not be asked to write letters slowly and painstakingly nor should the teacher demand immaculate copy-book work. Instead, each letter should be written scores of times with constant attention to the ease, speed and rhythm of production and to the quality of the letters written. Such practice can only be effective if it is adequately motivated by the desire to improve the qualities mentioned and if it is supervised and checked by the teacher. Undesirable departures from the basic form of the letters must be checked immediately they are observed and the pupil returned, if necessary, to practice with tactile letters.

(b) The Mechanics of Handwriting

Handwriting is a comparatively simple mechanical operation directed by the complex motor-muscular system of the writer; even the least able children usually learn to write after a fashion. Many children never reach a high degree of skill either because they do not attain the necessary degree of development of motor-muscular co-ordination or because insufficient attention has been given to the mechanical principles of handwriting movements. Unless the child is able to hold and move his pencil in such a way that free, fast-flowing, rhythmical and controlled movements are possible a high degree of skill is never reached. Even from the earliest stages, pupils must acquire as habits mechanically efficient methods of writing.

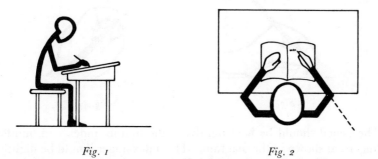

Fig. 1   Fig. 2

The child must be comfortably seated at a desk of the correct height in such a way that unrestricted movements of the writing hand and arm are facilitated. The teacher who does not attend to this seemingly obvious and elementary requirement handicaps her pupils and nullifies much of her instruction.

The desk and seat should be of such a height that when the pupil is seated as shown in the diagrams, the top of the desk is level with the lower ribs, the thighs are horizontal and the feet can be placed flat on the floor. The elbows should project about five centimetres over the edge of the desk which acts as a fulcrum for the forearm. If the desk is too high for the pupil the forearm will rest too firmly on the edge of the desk to permit free movement. Movement will also be restricted if the pupil crouches over the desk supporting part of the weight of his body on the forearms instead of entirely on his chair. The body should lean forward only very slightly as shown in the diagram so that the eyes are about twenty-five centimetres from the paper and the body is about six centimetres from the edge of the desk. For writing a sloping surface is to be preferred to a flat-topped desk or table, since it enables the pupils to see better what is being written and free writing movements are facilitated. The arms should be held easily and loosely so that free relaxed movements of the hands and arms are possible.

HOLDING THE PENCIL

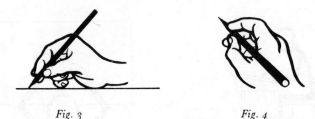

Fig. 3   *Fig. 4*

The pencil should be held lightly by the thumb, index and middle fingers, as shown in the diagram. The index finger should be slightly curved. The last two fingers of the hand may either rest lightly on the paper or be tucked comfortably out of the way. The ball of the hand may rest on the paper, but only very lightly, if at all, so that the hand can move easily over the surface of the paper. The hand should not be turned on its side nor should the wrist be in contact with the desk. The pencil should make an angle of about 45° with the plane of the paper and should point along the line of the forearm to beyond the right shoulder (see Fig. 2, page 15).

Because of the wide morphological differences in children, it would be unwise for the teacher to insist that every child should hold a pencil in exactly the same way or precisely as shown in the diagram. This is the manner in which the child should ultimately learn to hold the pencil. The teacher's efforts should be directed to guiding and encouraging the child to learn the correct method, and to ensuring that he does not develop wrong habits.

The chief errors to be guarded against in the early stages are gripping the pencil too tightly and pressing too heavily on the paper. The pencil should be held so lightly that the teacher can remove it from the pupil's hand with a gentle pull. Pupils may on occasion be asked to imagine that the pencil is a soft, downy feather and to hold it so lightly that it is not crushed.

Crooking of the forefinger is often a sign that the pencil is being held too tightly. The cure is to make the pupil hold the pencil with the thumb and middle finger and merely rest the forefinger on the pencil.

The use of short pieces of chalk or stubs of pencils cannot be too strongly deprecated for not only does the child have to hold these very tightly, but a most undesirable method of holding the pencil or chalk has to be adopted and this may become the established method of doing so.

FINGER, HAND AND ARM MOVEMENTS

In the early stages the infant will utilise the larger arm muscles in writing. The hand, wrist and fingers will be relaxed but play little part in moving the pencil to form letters and words. Pupils should be discouraged at any stage from attempting to move the pencil solely by flexure of the fingers.

A skilled writer by the middle of the primary stage is expected to write by almost imperceptible movements of the fingers and hand and by extensions and retractions of the hand from the wrist. The teacher must encourage this development as the child matures. The arm ceases to play a major part in the formation of letters and serves to carry the writing hand across the page. The writing arm can be

17

made to progress from left to right either by moving the whole arm in steps sideways as in Figure 5 or by moving the hand in an arc with its centre at a point in front of the elbow as shown in Figure 6. In either case the arm rests on the edge of the desk on the large muscle of the forearm. The first method is appropriate for young children and enables vertical pulled strokes towards the body to be made easily. In this case, the paper should be placed with its bottom edge parallel to the edge of the desk and, for the right-handed child, slightly to the right of the centre of the body.

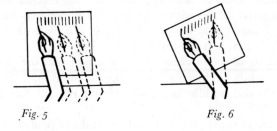

Fig. 5   Fig. 6

The second method should be used with older pupils as it facilitates the unrestricted speedy movement of the pencil across the page. In this case the pencil moves in a line which is slightly curved and inclined to the edge of the desk. If the page is wide, both forms of movement may have to be used. When the second method is used, the paper should be placed slightly to the right of the centre of the body and tilted slightly in the way shown so that the pencil moves in a path as nearly parallel as possible to the top edge of the paper. When the paper is tilted in this way the pulled strokes to the centre of the body will slope to the right as shown and sloping writing will be produced.

If a right-handed pupil writes with a backward slope it is because his posture is faulty or more commonly because he has turned his hand inward from the wrist so that the end of the pencil points to the right. In this position the pencil is pulled diagonally across the body instead of directly towards it. Writing produced by a flexing of the fingers instead of by small movements of the wrist, hand and fingers will also tend to slope backwards for the same reason.

18

Correct pencil-hold and the writing movement do not come naturally to a child, hence when picking up a tool, pencil or brush, the grasp is often tight, whereas writing should be done without pressure to prevent fatigue and to ensure free rhythmic movements. An anxiety to please the teacher and to make movements correctly causes tension and the hand becomes heavy. It is then that relaxation exercises are of use, but they need not be practised for a long time at each writing period. They can be practised at music or dancing times when rhythm and pleasure dominate the child's work.

All relaxation exercises must form a game so that the child is imagining a situation without being conscious of performing an action. There is a danger that formal instruction given to a child on the necessity of relaxing or on how to do so may achieve the opposite effect to that intended. With older children the teacher may, however, find it helpful on occasion to introduce pupils to exercises such as those listed below. They can be practised some time before they are required to be used in a lesson. When pupils are familiar with them and are aware of their purpose, they should be encouraged to use them, without instruction from the teacher, on each occasion they write, both before and during a spell of writing.

(1) Sit in writing position with arms dangling limply. Let hands flutter loosely when in this position.

(2) Lay forearms limply on the desk in the correct writing position. Raise and lower the elbows several times. Raise the forearms slightly with the desk edge serving as an axis, the hands hanging loosely and the finger-tips touching the desk.

(3) Place elbows on the desk with the forearms held upright. Let the hands flap loosely backwards and forwards while the fingers make slight snatching movements.

(4) Clench and unclench the fist repeatedly with the fingers spread.

(5) Drum lightly with fingers—' piano playing.'

(6) Circle hands inwards and outwards, then fling loosely sideways and downwards.

(c) *Fluency, Rhythm and Speed*

Fluent handwriting is writing in which the pencil does almost literally flow from letter to letter, from word to word and from one side of the page to the other in a smooth and almost continuous movement. Even single letters and unjoined print script can be written fluently.

Fluent writing need not be very speedy though it is generally more likely to be associated with writing produced at a reasonable speed than with slow, painstaking work. On the other hand speedy, regular writing is only likely to be obtained when it is produced fluently. Fluency comes from the response to rhythm, which in turn comes from ease of movement. The latter is only possible if a satisfactory mechanical system for writing has been acquired, hence the emphasis on correct posture, pencil-hold and relaxed muscles.

It will be found that fluency is the aspect of writing which probably gives most satisfaction to the young writer and this satisfaction of course plays a large part in contributing to permanent learning.

RHYTHM

Fluency comes from response to rhythm and ease of movement. The component parts of individual letters are written at different speeds and there is no regular, rhythmic beat in writing the letters in a word or words in a sentence. Fluent writing is however rhythmical in the sense that there is an absence of unnecessarily jerky or irregular movements. Parts of words at least are written with a smooth, steady and continuous movement and there is a regular progression from one such writing movement to the next.

The child should be accustomed from the beginning to the production of easy, rhythmic, free-flowing movements. He will be best able to do so if he is allowed to initiate his own movements and has not to conform too rigidly to the form of the model. It has been found that the learning of a motor skill such as writing is most rapid when the young learner is allowed to make free, easy movements which may be only partially correct in the early stages. Precision of movement is a relatively late development but with maturation and practice, jerky, irregular and unnecessary movements are eliminated and there is a gradual refinement in the form of the letters. Progress towards these ends will be most rapid if the insistence throughout has been on the rhythm of production.

The child will become familiar with and have much practice in making rhythmic movements during his singing games, dancing and singing, and during periods devoted to the making of movements with various parts of his body to the accompaniment of music with a marked rhythm. The earliest writing exercises may with advantage be made to the accompaniment of music, to rhythmical counting or to the repetition of a familiar nursery rhyme.

The work books and the sections dealing with details of the work to be attempted in the preparatory and infant stages contain many exercises of the following types. They serve the twofold purpose of giving pupils practice in writing rhythmically and in practising movements met with in their writing.

(1) Rhythmic patterns which progress across the page from left to right and are performed to the repetition of a nursery rhyme or to counting.

Jack and Jill went up the hill to fetch a pail of water

(2) Straight lines, ellipses, elements of letters and patterns performed (a) to descriptive naming of movements ; (b) to rhythmical counting ; (c) to music.

21

SPEED

Speed in writing is essential for the older pupil for in terms of its function, slow writing cannot be regarded as good or satisfactory writing. Speed alone, however, is not important and it must not be sought at the expense of legibility and general form. The pupil will only be able to write speedily and legibly when he has learned to write fluently. It must be realised that the writing of a letter slowly and carefully is a different thing from writing it quickly and almost automatically, for different neuromuscular reactions are involved. The process of writing slowly and painstakingly does not lead to the development of fluent writing but merely hardens into a habit of slow, laboured writing from which the pupil is unable to free himself without deterioration of letter forms.

From the earliest stages, therefore, the teacher must ensure that the pupil endeavours to write fluently, that is, rhythmically and at a reasonable speed. Although the child's movements are at first slow but rhythmical, they will be capable of increasing speed because they are rhythmical. Speed in writing must therefore be attained through the development and maintenance of rhythmic writing, and at no time should the child be pushed beyond his natural rate.

Speed tests play a valuable part in the upper primary classes in stimulating pupils to strive to increase the fluency of their writing. The standard method for testing the pupil's writing speed at these stages is to allow him to write the sentence, ' Mary had a little lamb,'

22

as often as he can in one minute. The number of *letters* written in one minute is the pupil's score.

Speed tests as such should be used with discretion in the infant stages, but the teacher may find it useful to use them very occasionally to assess the achievement and progress of pupils in the class. The results of such a test will at least make her vividly aware of the very wide range of abilities in pupils, for the scores at the end of the infant stage may well lie anywhere in the range of 5 to 100 letters per minute. For this reason it is impossible to give norms of writing speeds for this stage.

(d) Writing Exercises, Patterns and Designs

A young child takes delight in scribbling and drawing with pencil, chalk, crayon, brush or felt pen on cheap paper, newsprint or blackboards.

These informal exercises play a valuable part in developing control of the writing instrument.

The earliest exercises will be undirected scribbling, but even these can be made delightfully attractive by the use of colour to fill in spaces enclosed by the line made when the child ' takes the pencil for a walk.' It is during these early scribbling exercises that the child can be helped to hold a pencil correctly, to hold it lightly, and to practise writing lightly, smoothly, with relaxed and easy movements. Progress can soon be made to simple directed movements such as those which are suggested in the preceding section and in the scheme of lessons, where they are graded in difficulty.

From these early free writing activities should grow easily and naturally the writing of letter forms. The exercises should be such as to give pupils practice in making freely and rhythmically the movements involved in writing letters and should if possible be associated with familiar movements or presented in story form.

The making of these patterns will give further opportunities for the learning of the correct hold and method of use of the pencil. If the design is to be successful, much greater control will have to be exercised over the pencil but the movements should continue to be made rhythmically and smoothly and at reasonable speed, otherwise the exercise may do more harm than good.

At a later stage when letters have been learned, combinations of letters may be used to make patterns, thus giving much practice in writing This practice must be used with discretion, however, as deterioration of letter forms may pass unnoticed by the teacher, and undesirable methods of joining the letters may take place.

(e) Effective Practice

Improvement in a motor skill such as handwriting comes with maturation and practice, but it tends to appear in a series of steps. The child may remain at one level of achievement for quite a lengthy period and, in spite of the best endeavours of the teacher, fail to increase the fluency or improve the quality of his writing. Quite suddenly and unexpectedly, however, the child will come to write better in some way and this improvement will generally be maintained at about this level for another fairly lengthy period. Progress will continue to take place in a series of increases of skill, each alternating with a period of consolidation at the same level of achievement. During the period of little or no change the child may be unable to improve simply because his physical or neuromuscular organisation is incapable of giving a better performance. More generally, however, the limitation comes from lack of knowledge or understanding as to how the improvement may be achieved, from misdirected effort, or from relaxation of attention and effort to improve. The standard of performance may even decrease for a brief period immediately before improvement takes place due to new methods and knowledge being acquired and incompletely integrated with what was previously known and done. The rise from one plateau to another representing a higher level of achievement generally comes from a change of method when the physical organisation of the writer is sufficiently developed to permit further improvement. It comes when the mind grasps the significance of short cuts and of a better method of performance.

The significance of this for the teacher is that improvement can only happen if the child is consciously striving to improve, and has been shown and has understood what he must do to improve. Unless these conditions are fulfilled the rise from one level of achievement to a higher one is unlikely to take place. The longer a child practises at one level of achievement without making efforts to improve, the more firmly will his performance become established at that level and the more difficult it will be for him to become a better writer. Aimless practice of writing for the sake of writing or the production of pages

25

of writing without supervision from the teacher may be definitely harmful in that the performance of the writer may thereby tend to be consolidated at an unnecessarily low level.

Practice does not make perfect. Only adequately motivated and properly directed practice will lead to real improvement.

To sum up, if practice in writing is to be fully effective, the following conditions must be observed :

(1) Pupils must feel that it is important and worthwhile to improve their writing. They should consciously strive to do so each time they practise.

(2) Pupils must have a clear understanding of what they are expected to do to improve their writing. They should receive precise guidance as to the most effective methods of doing so.

(3) Practice must be directed to the achievement of a clearly defined and specific objective, e.g. the writing of a letter or word with increasing speed, rhythm and excellence of form.

(4) Practice either of a formal or informal kind must be purposive, meaningful, interesting and pleasurable. The feelings that accompany the acquisition of a skill play a big part in improving the level of performance.

(5) There must be short formal periods of specific instruction and practice in writing as distinct from other periods when writing is done in the service of other subjects.

(6) Frequent short periods of intensive formal practice are most effective. It is better to have a ten-minute lesson each day than to have one of fifty minutes once a week.

(7) When a pupil is writing a story or exercise his attention should be devoted in the first place to the subject matter rather than to the improvement of his writing. The lessons learned during the periods of formal instruction should, however, be reflected in the writing produced during such ordinary class work.

(8) The teacher must constantly observe *how* the child writes and make frequent checks on the quality and fluency of writing. Improvement in performance will be retarded no matter how hard a pupil strives if his writing techniques are faulty.

(9) The child must also be able to recognise and in time measure his standard of performance, for improvement in a skill is only likely to continue to increase when the performer is able to recognise rises in level of achievement.

(f) Forms of Instruction and Schemes of Work

INFORMAL INSTRUCTION

It has already been stressed that children learn to write most readily when what they write is satisfying, interesting and purposeful. Writing in the service of ordinary class work meets these requirements and so plays a major part in the instruction in handwriting and in giving necessary practice.

In general, practice in writing will be integrated with instruction in other subjects, and in particular will play an important part in the process of learning to read. Pupils will attempt to draw the letters, words and possibly short sentences they meet with in their early reading lessons, and copy the names, from cards, of familiar objects in the classroom. Before they have been taught to write, they may even reach that most exciting stage of being able to copy their own name from a card prepared by the teacher. When pupils learn to write by the methods advocated, they will continue to write words and sentences met with in reading lessons. They will also have much opportunity to practise by writing simple, short stories and descriptions and, at a later stage, in writing spelling words, geography, history and nature study notes. It is a basic precept that children should always be expected to read and check what they have written.

27

Pupils will have the opportunity, and indeed must be expected, to put into practice lessons they have learned during periods of more formal instruction. They should so understand the purpose of handwriting that they will strive to write well at all times and not merely regard legible and attractive handwriting as qualities demanded during formal periods of handwriting instruction.

In a sense, therefore, every time a child writes can be regarded as a lesson in handwriting. If, however, a child is to write happily, rejoicing in his ability to tell a story or to express his thoughts in writing, nothing should hinder the outpouring of his ideas.

If his whole conscious attention is to be devoted to the words he has to write and to the thoughts he wishes to express, he must not be expected to pay more than the bare minimum of attention to the writing process itself, nor must he be subject to frequent interruption or correction by the teacher. Gross faults of posture and of the mechanics of writing, however, must always receive immediate attention.

FORMAL INSTRUCTION

Since the occasional instruction given during the writing activities described above has the advantage of being adequately motivated, it plays a vital part in the teaching of handwriting. Such instruction is, however, obviously neither sufficiently systematic nor comprehensive. If handwriting is regarded as a motor skill, the mechanics of handwriting, the learning of letters and combinations of letters as patterns of movement and the intensive practice necessary for the development of skill in making these movements must receive adequate attention.

The periods of formal instruction must be brief since the young child co-ordinates imperfectly and therefore tires easily, and because of the difficulty of sustaining interest in formal exercises. In the early stages, frequent lessons of ten to fifteen minutes' duration are likely to be most effective.

These short formal lessons should be devoted to teaching the basic handwriting techniques, the correct method of forming a new letter and practice in writing fluently and correctly a particular letter which has already been learned. The writing of groups of letters, words and sentences with increasing speed, rhythm and excellence, the performance of rhythm and pattern-making exercises, training in correct posture, pencil-hold and relaxation and the assessment of speed and quality of writing, are all aspects of the subject which should receive attention during these periods.

It is essential that formal instruction be made interesting and meaningful for the pupil. He should not only know precisely what he has to do and how to do it but also why he is expected to do the exercise. The child will take delight in performing formal exercises and in striving to increase his skill if he understands the purpose of the exercise and is expected to make use of the skill he acquires in the service of his ordinary class work. Interest will be sustained and progress be most rapid when pupils are able to note improvements in their own efforts. It should be remembered, however, that the ability of pupils in the class will vary within wide limits and the stimulant of praise should not be reserved only for pupils who reach the highest standards.

The brief periods of formal instruction can often usefully be followed by a short exercise in writing interesting and meaningful material during which time the child will be expected to put into practice the lessons he has just learned. Writing of an ordinary class exercise can often with advantage be preceded by brief reminders about correct posture, pencil-hold, relaxation, and by the performance of a rhythmical pattern-exercise learned during the formal writing lesson.

The schemes of work contained in Part Two of this book are mainly devoted to the work to be attempted during these periods of formal instruction. It is not intended that teachers adhere rigidly to these schemes, or use every exercise exactly in the order or manner set down. They provide a framework for systematic, formal instruction covering the two years in the infant rooms, explain and illustrate techniques, methods and principles, and contain exercises of various kinds suited to each stage of instruction.

(g) Left-Handed Pupils

There is no clear-cut distinction of pupils as either right-handed or left-handed. Margaret Clark * states that although about 8 per cent of boys and 6 per cent of girls were found in her investigations to write with the left hand, these numbers represent only a fraction of the pupils with left-hand tendencies. Some children with a left-hand preference change to the use of the right hand for writing when they begin to receive instruction in school or even before they enter school.

Although the degree of tendency to use the right or left hand varies greatly, not only in individuals, but also in the task which is attempted, it is found that right- or left-hand dominance for writing is almost invariably established before a child enters school.

No attempt should be made to force or even to persuade a left-handed pupil to write with the right hand. The writing produced by a left-handed pupil need not be inferior in any way to that of the right-handed pupil. The left-handed pupil is likely to become a more skilled writer if he is taught how to write with his left hand than if forced to use the right hand and employ writing techniques appropriate only to the use of that hand.

Nervous and emotionally unstable children who are left-handed may suffer positive harm if forceful measures are used to achieve a change to right-handedness. It is, however, essential that the left-handed pupil be given instruction suited to his particular needs if he is to learn to write with grace and skill.

On the other hand it would be folly to permit children to write with either hand at will. Writing which progresses from left to right has been evolved because it entails movements which are natural and easy for the right-handed. The left-handed writer also meets the difficulties explained below which are not experienced by the right-handed child. The teacher, therefore, must insist that right-handed children and those whose hand preference is slight or doubtful should write with the right hand.

* *Teaching Left-handed Children*, by Margaret M. Clark, Scottish Council for Research in Education, XLIV. University of London Press, 1960

The infant teacher's first task must be to determine, on the basis of a careful diagnosis, the child's hand preference. It is necessary that a number of different tests be given to each child since hand preference appears to vary for different activities. It is also important that the child should not be aware that he is being tested for right- or left-handedness.

Tests such as the following will be found to be effective. Observation is made of the hand used in the activity and of the skill in using the preferred and non-preferred hand.

Picking up a pencil or piece of chalk placed centrally before the
    child on his desk and writing and drawing with it.
Throwing a ball into a box.
Catching with one hand a ball thrown by the teacher.
Sharpening a pencil. (The preferred hand holds the knife.)
Sorting blocks into a box.
Threading a bead.
Holding a bat.
Using a hammer.
Brushing the teeth or hair.
Stirring.
Screwing a cap on a bottle.
Cutting paper with scissors.
Reaching for an object.
Building beakers.
Using a screw toy.

Margaret Clark details some of these tests and gives a ' Speed of crossing ' test which indicates the relative ability of the two hands.*

Pupils who are left-handed, or who are found by such tests to have a fair degree of left-handed preference, must not only be permitted to write with the left hand but must be shown how to do so to the best advantage.

The teacher cannot give adequate help to such pupils unless she is aware of the following difficulties they must surmount :

* Op. cit. page 42

(1) The arm of the right-handed person can move easily across the desk and away from the body, but the arm used by the left-handed writer is restricted in movement by having to move across and towards the body. The natural writing movement for a left-handed writer would be across the page from right to left.

(2) The hand holding the writing instrument moves over the top of the words which are being written and therefore hides and may smudge them.

(3) Joining strokes between letters have to be made with a pushed instead of a sidled movement. If a sharp-pointed writing instrument is used, it will not move easily over the writing surface and may even stick into it.

The following procedure is recommended for teaching left-handed pupils at all stages :

(1) Grossly unorthodox postures are quite unnecessary and must not be permitted. The pupil should be seated comfortably in a relaxed position, exactly as for a right-handed child. The body may be turned slightly to the right so as to give the left arm more freedom of movement, but the left elbow should not rest on the desk.

(2) The writing paper or exercise book should be placed slightly to the left of the centre of the body and at a later stage may be tilted to the right as shown in the diagram. This may result in the development of a slight backward slope but this should be tolerated in the case of left-handed writers.

(3) The writing instrument must be held lightly in the left hand in a manner corresponding to that illustrated as appropriate for a right-handed pupil but it may be held slightly farther from the point than usual (about 3 cm) to enable the child to see what he has written. The pencil should point along the line of the forearm.

(4) The left-handed child is bound to be aware that he is different from the majority of his fellow pupils, but the teacher should never draw attention to this difference. He is likely to find the task of learning to write more difficult than it is for a right-handed child and will need the sympathetic encouragement of his teacher at all stages.

In the early infant stages it may be necessary to give much preliminary practice in making scribbling patterns of a large size which progress from left to right across the page or blackboard.

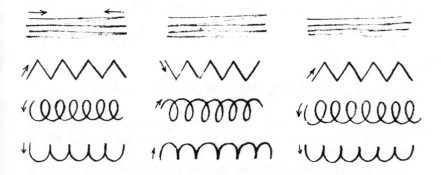

Particular attention should be paid to the ease and rhythm of production. The tracing of letters and the frequent use of tactile letters will also help in the early stages. The teacher must always be alert to detect any tendency to mirror-writing or reversals in the early stages.

A tendency to mirror-writing is potentially present in a left-handed child. Although mirror-writing has a higher incidence among mentally defective children than among normal, it is not an indication of mental retardation except when it continues in an older child as his only, or usual, form of writing.

The production of mirror-writing by a left-handed child in the early stages of learning to write need cause the teacher no great concern or difficulty if immediate steps are taken to prevent it from becoming a habit. Mirror-writing can only be produced if the pupil starts at the right-hand side of the page and then writes from right to left. To prevent this, a device such as marking the starting place with a cross can be used. The child should be made aware that the writing he produces is different from normal writing and he should be given practice in writing slowly, carefully and correctly from a copy. The tracing of letters and the use of tactile letters will also be found to help in the eradication of the tendency to mirror-writing.

A fuller explanation of this aspect of the work is given by Clark.*

(h) Writing Materials and Work Books

The writing materials which have been found most useful at each stage of instruction are noted in the appropriate sections of the Schemes of Work.

In general, the writing instruments and surfaces used should be such that the child can make easy, free-flowing movements to produce letters of a size in keeping with his degree of neuromuscular development.

Thus, in the earliest stages, large sheets of cheap paper such as blank newsprint, wrapping paper or thin sugar paper can be used

* Op. cit. page 15

with felt pens, giant crayons or brushes with thin poster colour. Individual blackboards and chalk are used in many infant rooms and provide a cheap and convenient method of obtaining frequent practice in making patterns and in writing letters and words. Such blackboards must be reasonably large and have a good, smooth surface. The child should not be allowed to make small, cramped writing or be permitted to write with small pieces of chalk.

Coloured pastels are not suitable for use by infants as they are messy, break too easily and are too thin and too short to be held in the desired manner. Coloured pencils are a useful tool since they are a cheap and convenient means of making coloured patterns and illustrations, but they suffer from the disadvantages of having a thin stem, of accustoming the pupil to press too firmly on the paper and of requiring frequent re-sharpening.

Towards the end of the preparatory period, a pencil with a thick stem and a soft, thick, black lead is recommended as the most convenient and suitable instrument for most of the writing the child is asked to perform. Most pencil manufacturers produce this type of pencil.

An ordinary pencil with a slim, polished stem has to be held tightly by the young child if adequate control is to be maintained. Undesirable habits of holding and using the pencil may develop for this reason. A light plastic holder about 12 cm long and 1 cm wide enables young children to hold an ordinary pencil more easily and prevents the distortion of the grip which occurs when a short pencil is used.

As a considerable amount of practice is needed in writing letters and words, in pattern-making and in rhythm and fluency exercises, especially during the periods of formal instruction, loose sheets of cheap paper will prove to be more convenient and economical than writing books. Books should, however, be used from an early stage for informal work and for the writing of patterns, letters and words that have already been practised. Each child should have his own book with his name written by the teacher on the cover. The first book should consist of not more than a dozen pages of cheap paper such as newsprint, measuring about 35 × 25 cm stapled or sewn into a cover of brown paper or sugar paper. Giant wax crayons, felt pens or thick pencils are best used with this book.

When the first book is completed, a smaller one measuring about 25 × 20 cm should be used in which the pupils write their short stories and combine writing and illustrations. It could consist of better paper than the first but again should not contain too many pages. Thick pencils and coloured pencils should be used.

As the child's skill increases, writing books can become progressively smaller. By the middle of the second year in the infant room, a book measuring about 20 × 15 cm is large enough for children of average ability.

Writing books should be unruled, have few pages, and have an attractive cover of card or stiff paper on which is written the child's name and the topic, e.g. Our school ; My class book ; My news book ; The playpark book ; Pets, etc.

BLANK OR RULED PAPER

It is fairly general practice in infant rooms to use blank paper for all forms of writing exercises, as it enables the child to write freely and rhythmically letters of a size in keeping with his stage of neuro-muscular development.

Paper which is ruled with single or multiple lines might seem at first to ease the task of the teacher and pupil as linearity and spacing of writing, uniformity of letter size and letters of the correct relative height can fairly readily be obtained by its use. But in the long run it is neither necessary nor desirable. Experience shows that the great majority of young children have little trouble with the alignment of their writing if due attention is given to correcting posture. Uniformity of size of letters in the early stages is neither to be expected nor demanded. Children will, when they are able, tend to make their writing of the same size as the samples written by the teacher and that illustrated in the work books. It is doubtful if multiple rulings really help children to learn more readily the relative heights of letters. Indeed there is some evidence to show that the masking of writing by multiple rulings hinders the development of the ability to appreciate and write letters of the correct relative size. Occasionally, children even develop habits of faulty letter formation through having to conform to rulings unsuited to their stage of development.

Blank paper can be used with success and advantage in every class throughout the school. Not only does its use facilitate the development of fluent and rhythmical writing and an early appreciation of correct size and spacing of letters and words, but children using it find pleasure and satisfaction in their work. They welcome the emancipation from the restriction of lines and the freedom to set out their work according to their own tastes and abilities. The care and attention they are required to exercise during their writing lessons is reflected in the neatness and arrangement of all their written work.

WORK BOOKS

The two infant Work Books illustrate some of the work to be attempted during the short daily periods of formal instruction in the infant classes. Prototypes of the lower-case letters, capitals and numerals are illustrated and their method of construction indicated. Numerous examples of rhythm and pattern-making exercises, simple words, sentences allied to illustration and continuous passages of writing are provided for guidance and practice.

Each exercise should be performed by the children over and over again until the desired degree of speed, rhythm and quality is attained The schemes of work in Part Two of this book contain page by page reference to the Work Books and give detailed instructions for their use.

Although the Work Books illustrate material which may also be used during the more informal periods of writing, they must certainly not be regarded as providing a complete course in the teaching of handwriting. It must again be emphasised that they provide material mainly for the short intensive periods of formal instruction which is an essential but comparatively minor part of the instruction in writing at infant stage.

4

Letter Forms and Styles

The letter forms which are illustrated in this scheme and in the Work Books are the prototypes of our traditional and satisfying forms. ' The unchangeable, significant letter forms which continue to serve our purpose best today are so established within our civilisation that we cannot tamper with them ; it is not possible to devise a new basic form : we can only accept what history gives us.' *

CHOICE OF LETTER FORMS

Many minor variations of the elementary letter forms used in this scheme are in current use, but for the purpose of illustrations in the Work Books it was necessary to choose and adhere to one particular form for each letter. The choice was made by a panel of experienced teachers with the following considerations in mind :

(1) The basic, elementary form of each letter without adult conceptions of stylisation and final form must be the one which is presented to the young pupil.

(2) The letters must be simple, legible and pleasing, and be capable of continuous development into a more mature form without losing these characteristics.

(3) It is wasteful of time and effort to teach print script to infants and then to change to a different style of writing in the primary classes. The letter forms used should be capable of continuous development without major change.

(4) As far as their structure permits, the letters should be capable of being written in one smooth, continuous movement so that they can be readily taught and learned as patterns of movement.

* *Primary Education*, H.M.S.O., 1959, p. 249

38

(5) The bodies of the letters *a*, *b*, *c*, *d*, *g*, *o*, *p* and *q* should be oval or elliptical as the ellipse can be made more easily and fluently than a circle or the somewhat triangular shape characteristic of some forms of modern italic.

(6) All letters should be capable of being written rhythmically and fluently at all stages of instruction and so form the foundation for an extremely speedy and fluent adult hand.

Some schools may wish to use particular letters slightly different from those illustrated in the scheme. There is no reason why they should not do so as long as the above considerations are kept in mind and there is uniformity of style throughout the school ; but if changes are made from the letter forms illustrated difficulties may arise in the use of the pupils' Work Books.

INDIVIDUALITY OF STYLE

It is not intended that pupils at any stage should be required to make exact reproductions of the letters and writing illustrated in the scheme and the Work Books. These letters are the basic, skeletal forms from which each child's personal style should derive. ' From the moment an infant grasps a pencil to write, he makes shapes which are peculiarly his own.' * The prototype letters illustrated are so simple that an infinite number of acceptable variations is possible, and the child's own individual style of letter may well have a pleasing grace and quality, due to the fluency and rhythm of production, which is lacking in the formal, carefully drawn prototype. Major departures from the basic form of the letter, exaggeration of specific features, or a tendency to unnecessary flourishes or ornamentation must of course be prohibited.

The infant teacher should keep constantly in mind that what is required at this stage is easy rhythmical movement of writing rather than the accuracy and uniformity of letter form appropriate to a later stage of instruction.

* *Twentieth Century Handwriting*, by V. E. C. Gordon and Ruth Mock. Methuen 1960

All the children in one class should not be asked or expected to produce exactly the same size of letters. The size should be related to the pupil's stage of neuromuscular development and co-ordination and to the writing instrument used. In general a pupil will progress from fairly large letters to smaller ones as the control of the finer movements of the pencil by the fingers and hand develops.

A pupil who has reached this latter stage of muscular development will be inhibited from developing a fluent hand if he is continually forced to make larger letters than need be the case. On the other hand pupils tend to write smaller letters than they ought since they wish to write like older children and adults. By writing smaller than their stage of development justifies, incorrectly shaped letters and even illegible writing lacking in rhythm of production will result.

In general, a child is likely to write with the desired degree of fluency and rhythm only when the size of the letters he uses is in keeping with his stage of development.

The letters and writing illustrated in the Work Books gradually decrease in size from the first Infant Work Book to Primary Work Book 4. The size of writing used in each book is based on what has been found to be fairly common usage for that stage, but it will be clear that these sizes are intended only as a guide as to what might be expected on the average at a particular stage.

GROUPING OF LETTERS

The lower-case letters shown opposite are arranged in five groups according to the movements required to write them and this form of classification has been adopted throughout the scheme of work. All letters do not, however, fall into strictly defined groups and there is no reason why a teacher should not adopt a grouping which better suits her purpose.

The starting point and the movement required to construct each lower-case letter and capital are shown on page 44.

o c a d g q u
e s f l i t j k
b p n m h r
v w x y z

Pulled strokes are used in preference to pushed strokes.
f, i, j, t, k, x and *y* are made with two strokes. All other
small letters are made with one continuous movement.

PROPORTIONS AND RELATIVE HEIGHTS

To simplify instruction, young pupils can be told that ascenders and
descenders are about twice the size of the small letters. Ideally
capitals and ascenders should be slightly smaller than twice the
height of the small letters and the tails of descenders slightly less

than the height of a small letter, but young pupils are unable to
appreciate such fine distinctions and should not be burdened with
rules of this kind. They should not, however, be allowed to make
ascenders too tall and the tails of descenders too long. From the
earliest stages they should learn to make the letters *f* and *t* inter-
mediate in height between the small letters and tall ascenders.

Capitals vary greatly in width. For the guidance of teachers the approximate proportions are as shown.

W *width nearly one and a half times the height*

M *width about the same as the height*

ACGOQ *width a little over three-quarters the height*

DHKNTUVXYZ

width about two-thirds the height

BEFJLPRS *width about half the height*

The cross strokes of *P* and *R* intersect at the mid height of the letters ; those of *B*, *E*, *F* and *H* slightly above the half-way line, and that of *A* slightly below. Children, of course, should not be asked to learn these proportions. They will in time come to know when the letter is correctly made if they use the Work Books and tactile letters and if they see correctly proportioned letters on the teacher's blackboard.

42

For the guidance of the teacher the recognised rules for letter spacing are summarised below :

(1) Wide spacing—when two vertical strokes come together :

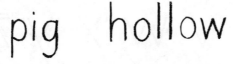

will limit jump

(2) Medium spacing—when an oval letter and a vertical stroke are adjacent :

pig hollow

(3) Narrow spacing—when two oval letters are adjacent :

good dog

Pupils should merely be asked to write letters fairly close together without touching each other and told that all spaces between letters should look the same. If the letters are correctly spaced the visual distance between all letters in a word will appear the same even though their actual distances are different.

The rules for the spacing of capitals are approximately the same, e.g. HILL *not* HILL.

Words should be spaced so that they are distinguishable as separate parts of a sentence. In the earliest stages of writing with a pencil the width of the point of the forefinger between words is a commonly used measure. By the end of the infant stage the width of a capital *O* between words is a suitable measure and in the late primary stage the width of a small *o* or *a* is appropriate.

a b c d e f g h i j k
l m n o p q r s t
u v w x y z

A B C D E F G
H I J K L M N
O P Q R S T U
V W X Y Z

Numerals

The prototypes illustrated below are based mainly on the recommendations made in the report by the Scottish Council for Research in Education on the teaching of numerals.* They have been chosen from many possible varying forms so as to emphasise the essential form of each numeral as revealed by its history, for their stability, for their distinctiveness and so that they may not readily be confused with other numerals. All the numerals are the same size.

Method of Construction

0 Oval—not circular

1 Simple vertical stroke

2 Single curve and straight base. The distinctive element is the turn—not the head or stem.

3 The central turn is the emphatic element. The upper curve is slightly smaller than the lower.

4 The proportion of the parts is relatively unimportant if the cross stroke is made boldly and crosses the horizontal.

5 May be written with a horizontal attached flag or a detached flag at an angle of 45°.

6 May be written either in a clockwise or anti-clockwise direction. The loop is not closed. The relative size of the loop and the terminal curve are of minor importance as long as extremes are avoided.

7 Flat top and angular turn.

8 May be written by starting at the top with an anti-clockwise motion, or by beginning with a right-to-left downstroke. The latter method is better for a number of reasons. The top of the number may be left unclosed.

9 The printed form of this numeral if written with a clockwise motion has certain advantages. The form illustrated here is more commonly used and is probably preferable, if it is learned and written in one continuous movement.

---

* *The Writing of Arabic Numerals*, by Dr G. G. Neill Wright, University of London Press Ltd., 1955

In the infant classes the emphasis must be on the rhythmical production of letter forms of reasonable quality based on the prototype letters illustrated. The unjoined script used for class work must also be written with considerable fluency and rhythm. Perfection of letter forms appropriate to a later stage of development must not be sought by slow copying of shapes at the expense of ease and rhythm of movement.

At the beginning of the primary stage pupils learn to terminate with incipient ligatures certain of the letters learned in the infant room. When the child is writing fluently these incipient ligatures are carried to the beginning of the next letter so that the two letters are written together as a complete rhythmical whole. Other forms of ligaturing are learned at later stages, but ligatures are used only when they come easily and naturally and have been found to aid the fluency and rhythm of writing without impairing its legibility.

At all stages fluent rather than speedy writing is sought. Letter forms, although basically the same as those learned in the infant room, improve in quality and grace through the maturation of the writer and the increasing fluency and rhythm of production. In the third primary class writing with pen and ink is introduced. At first unshaded writing is used, but in the fourth primary class square-edged pens can be introduced to give a very attractive shaded style of writing, again without change of the basic form of letters learned in the infant room. The appearance of the writing used in successive primary classes is illustrated on pages 49–52.

The scheme of work and methods of instruction used at the primary stage are described in the *Teacher's Book—Primary*. The formal work and exercises to be attempted at this stage are illustrated in Work Books 1, 2, 3 and 4.

b p n m h r

mother mother

apple apple

run run run run

bell bell bell

pram pram

CROSS HERE

WAIT

HALT STOP

SLOW

HOSPITAL

SCHOOL

KEEP LEFT

Specimen page from Work Book B, Infant Scheme

If I were an apple

If I were an apple
    And grew upon a tree
I think I'd fall down
    On a nice boy like me.

I wouldn't stay there
    Giving nobody joy;
I'd fall down at once
    And say "Eat me my boy.

151, Abbey Street,
Eastown,
1st April, 1960

Dear John,

I am learning to write both quickly and well.

I must be able to write quickly so that my writing will help me with other lessons such as spelling, sums, writing letters and exercises.

It is also important to write clearly and well, so that others can read my writing easily.

Your friend,
Tom Brown

Specimen page from Work Book 2, Primary Scheme

45 Castle Road
Bridgetown
4th January 1961

Dear Mary,

Since my last letter to you I have been learning to write with pen and ink.

When you are writing in ink you must be very sure that you are holding your pen correctly. If you do that you will find it just as easy to write quickly and well with a pen as with a pencil.

Your sincere friend,

Jane Smith

Think On These Things

Whatsoever things are true,
whatsoever things are honest,
whatsoever things are just,
whatsoever things are pure,
whatsoever things are lovely,
whatsoever things are of
good report,
if there be any virtue
and if there be any praise
think on these things.

PART TWO

SCHEMES OF WORK

I

The Preparatory Period

INTRODUCTION

It has been explained in Part One of this book that children entering school vary widely in physical and mental development and that few are ready to profit immediately from formal instruction in handwriting. A preparatory period is, therefore, necessary during which the teacher will be able to observe the child, assess his ability and stage of development, and provide activities designed to promote readiness for writing.

The duration of this preparatory stage and the nature and extent of the instruction to be given will be determined by the capabilities and needs of individual children.

The activities which are listed below are not to be regarded as a scheme of work ; they are merely indicative of the type of work appropriate to this stage of instruction. The teacher will probably wish to add to the activities and exercises listed and employ those she finds most effective, bearing in mind that the work arranged for each child is determined by his needs. Even at this stage the teacher may find it desirable to group children for instructional purposes.

During the preparatory stage, the work of the teacher will include the following :

(1) Observation of individual pupils and assessment of their abilities and stage of development as shown by their behaviour and performance during class activities.

(2) The determination of the degree of right or left-handed preference of individual pupils and the decision as to whether or not a child should write with the left hand (see page 30).

(3) Directing of play activities and exercises to develop control of the larger muscles : throwing, rolling, catching and bouncing balls ; skipping ; dancing ; running and jumping to music ; climbing with agility apparatus ; hammering ; games and play activities which involve large arm movements such as pretending to be windmills, trains, or branches of trees in the wind.

(4) Directing activities to exercise the smaller muscles of the hand and fingers and to develop co-ordination of hand and eye : folding paper ; pricking and cutting out shapes and cut-outs ; recognising shapes and fitting templates and geometric figures into frames ; building and stacking with bricks and beakers ; using screw toys and peg boards ; modelling with clay or plasticine ; drawing in sand ; games, mime and play activities involving finger and wrist movements ; scribbling and drawing on blackboards with chalk or on large sheets of paper with felt pen or paint brush ; tracing with transparent paper over letters and pictures ; playing with tactile letters and jigsaws.

(5) Giving miming exercises to relax muscles : washing, wringing, rubbing, shaking and folding clothes ; brushing hair ; stroking a cat ; playing a piano or violin ; picking up and pushing gently a feather ; catching soap bubbles or snowflakes ; throwing up a balloon ; picking up sweets and putting them in a dish.

(6) Giving initial guidance towards the correct method of holding and using a writing instrument, and help in acquiring postures facilitating unrestricted writing movements (see pages 15 to 18).

(7) Presenting reading activities prior to formal instruction in writing. Success in learning to write is dependent upon the ability to differentiate between letter forms and to be able to read even to a limited degree. Activities will include the use of sensory apparatus such as tactile letters as an aid to the perception of specific letter-shapes met with in reading lessons and later in writing lessons. Pupils should be encouraged to attempt to draw letters, words and even sentences met in the reading lessons. As

the occasion arises, instruction should be given to pupils in the correct method of writing the letters they are attempting to draw.

(8) Giving practice in writing movements using paint brushes, felt pens and chalk, and finally thick pencils. Undirected scribbling movements and shading using these instruments are followed by simple directed movements and rhythmical pattern exercises and exercises involving the use of letter elements. Even during this stage, pupils who are able should be encouraged to copy meaningful words, phrases and sentences met with in the reading lessons and on cards attached to objects in the room. The emphasis throughout this stage is on ease and rhythm of production and on the feel of the movement when writing, rather than on the excellence of the form of what is produced.

SUMMARY OF WRITING ACTIVITIES

(1) Writing movements using paint brushes, felt pens or chalk.

(2) Scribbling exercises with pencil.

(3) Recognising shapes and filling in outlines with coloured pencils.

(4) Rhythmic writing exercises to counting, music and rhymes.

(5) Writing movements with pencil making elements of letters, figures and patterns.

(6) Copying of letters, words and sentences.

The exercises which follow under these separate headings are not intended as a rigid scheme of work which must be followed. Rather they are to be regarded as suggestions to the teacher as to what may be attempted according to the size of class, the ability of the pupils, the size and nature of the classroom and the availability of materials.

Stories should be woven round each exercise no matter how simple it is, to give it purpose and to add to the child's pleasure in the activity. Where possible each child should be allowed to collect his own material and return it to the correct cupboard at the end of the lesson.

(1) *Writing movements using a paint brush*

Materials. Jars of ready-mixed poster colours, hog hair brushes No. 8 or 10—long handles—round or flat, sheets of sugar paper.

Pupils can also repeat the exercises later using blackboards and coloured chalk.

(a) Green field with flowers. Begin the lesson with a relaxation exercise, e.g. pupils pretend they are picking flowers from a field with delicate, relaxed movements of finger and wrist. Follow with a painting lesson where the children lift their brushes as if they were lifting fragile flowers. They continue to hold and use them lightly while they cover their sheets of paper with green paint to represent a field. Spots of white or coloured paint are added to represent flowers.

While the children are painting, move around the class and assist pupils who have difficulty in holding or manipulating the brush or paint and correct pupils who have adopted unnatural or awkward postures.

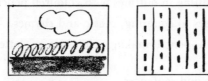 

(b) The Seaside. Sky, sea, waves, sand—scribbling strokes, lines and flat wash of colour. Preliminary relaxation exercise—moving the arms and hands gently to and fro like waves.

(c) Wallpaper. Long and short vertical strokes in various colours.

(d) Blue pond with paths round it. Begin path and pond at top right-hand corner and move anticlockwise. The picture can be completed by adding patches of colour to represent trees in the park. Preliminary relaxation exercise—full arm circling in anti-clockwise direction with hand and fingers hanging loosely.

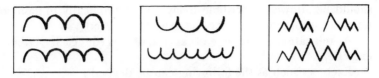

(e) Bridges, or boy hopping, etc. Clockwise movement—up—over —down. Relaxation exercise—making bridges in the air with wrists and fingers relaxed.

(f) Waves on the sea or skipping. Relaxation exercise—arms making swaying movements up and down.

(g) Climbing up and down mountains. Relaxation exercise—with the muscles of the arms, wrists, and fingers loose, flap hands up and down.

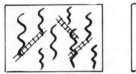 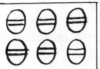 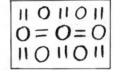

(h) Snakes and ladders. Show children how to fill page with curves of various colours and sizes. Add ladders if desired. Relaxation exercise—arms hanging loosely from the shoulder, let hands and fingers flutter limply.

(i) Coloured Easter eggs in a box. Paint eggs of various colours with coloured bands round them. Relaxation exercise—with elbows resting on the desk, rotate hands from the wrist.

(j) Pattern. Show children how to fill the page with a pattern of ovals and straight lines. Relaxation exercise—with fingers loose, pretend to play the piano on the surface of the desk.

(2) *Scribbling exercises with pencil*

A pencil with a thick soft lead should be used and the child taught how to hold it lightly in a reasonably correct manner. The exercises should be done on sheets of cheap blank paper such as newsprint, and each exercise should be performed many times. The child should be allowed to scribble freely and rhythmically to gain confidence and practice in using the new tool correctly.

A relaxation exercise can as usual precede each scribbling exercise.

Exercises such as the following can be devised :

Smoke from a bonfire. Draw a small pile of sticks
to represent a bonfire and fill the page with scribbles to
represent smoke. The important aspect of the exercise,
is how it is performed rather than the quality of the
finished product.

In a similar manner pupils may make scribbling lines to represent clouds, dust billowing from behind a vehicle, waves and spray, a fountain playing, waterfalls and rapids, a ball bouncing or rolling, a piece of paper blown by the wind, fireworks, a wheel turning.

An exercise which will be enjoyed by the children is commonly known as ' taking the pencil for a walk '. The pencil makes a continuous line as in the diagrams below.

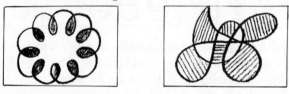

The enclosed spaces can be shaded in with crayons of various colours to make an attractive pattern.

(3) *Recognising shapes and filling in outlines*

Sensory materials such as Montessori insets, wood and cardboard shapes and profiles of trees, flowers, leaves, animals, letters and numbers which are normally found in infant classrooms can be used with advantage at this stage. Children handle these materials and move a finger round the edge to feel the shape. They are then provided with sheets of cheap paper and pencils, crayons or coloured pencils with which they draw round the shape. The outline thus drawn can then be filled in with coloured pencil. When one outline has been filled in, the children may be allowed to choose other insets and fill their paper or a page of their large writing books with coloured shapes. Children should not be asked to trace round small or intricate shapes, nor should they be allowed to use small stubs of crayons or pencil.

(4) *Rhythmic writing patterns to music, rhyme or counting*

Children who have performed the exercises detailed in the earlier sections, should now be beginning to sit correctly when writing and be better able to use a pencil in a reasonably satisfactory manner. Attention must now be placed increasingly on the ease and rhythm of writing. The following exercises will give pleasure to the child and help to impress on him the need to move his pencil smoothly and steadily when he writes. The teacher must recognise that in the early stages it is as important to watch the writer and how he writes as it is to pay attention to what he writes.

These exercises can be used with advantage at all stages of instruction throughout the school. The pupils' Work Books and the scheme for the infant stages contain many additional examples.

(*a*) Rhythmic patterns which progress across the page from left to right and are performed to the repetition of a nursery rhyme or to counting. The five patterns illustrated below give practice in making all the movements used in writing.

Jack and Jill went up the hill
to fetch a pail of water ;

Jack fell down and broke his crown,
and Jill came tumbling after.

The exercise can also be performed to a steady repetition of 'one, two,' where the downstroke is made on the count of one and the up-stroke on the count of two. If a rhyme is used, each stroke can be associated with a monosyllable but a very precise metrical correspondence need not be sought. As long as the children say the verse steadily and write fluently and rhythmically as they repeat the words, the purpose of the exercise will be served.

61

Mary, Mary quite contrary, etc.

Humpty Dumpty sat on a wall, etc.

Dickory, Dickory, Dock, etc.

One two, buckle my shoe, etc.

(*b*) Straight lines, ellipses, letters and patterns performed to descriptive naming of the movements, to rhythmical counting or to music.

Up, down, etc. or 1, 2, 1, 2.

The simplest of these exercises is the repetition of a straight up and down movement on one line. This type of exercise can be performed to the naming of the movements, to counting or to music. It will be found to be particularly useful in helping children to develop a sense of rhythm in making writing movements. The exercise, illustrated on the right, of running the pencil or the finger continuously up and down against a straight edge such as a book, board or ruler, will be found helpful particularly with the less able children. These exercises should be performed frequently for short periods at a time until the child can make the movement speedily, confidently and rhythmically.

The exercise can then be varied by making the strokes to a specific count or by allowing the strokes to progress across the page :

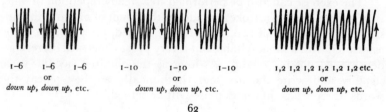

1–6	1–6	1–6	1–10	1–10	1–10	1,2 1,2 1,2 1,2 1,2 1,2 etc.
or			or			or
down up, down up, etc.			down up, down up, etc.			down up, down up, etc.

62

Exercises such as these can be made to a count of one for each separate stroke up or down or to a count of one for each combined up and down stroke, depending on the speed and rhythm with which the pupils are able to write. The aim is to maintain a steady, rhythmical movement. Similarly for the continuous ellipses illustrated below it will be necessary to adjust the count according to the size of the ellipse, the skill of the pupils and the tempo desired. Thus in the earliest stages, each ellipse may have to be made to a count of four or to a naming movement such as over, down, round, up.

1,2 1,2 1,2 for each
elipse or *down up, down up*, etc.

1–10   1–10   1–10
Complete elipse to each count of one, or *down and down*, etc.

It should be borne in mind that the establishment of a fluent, rhythmical movement rather than precision or excellence of form must be the first objective. Before the child writes on paper, he can learn the movement and establish rhythm in making it by writing with his finger in the air or on the desk, by sliding the blunt end of his pencil on the desk or paper. When he is familiar with the movement, the pencil can be lowered and the exercise begun with a ' running start '.

On occasion, exercises such as those illustrated in this section may be performed to music with a well-defined beat, but as there is likely to be a wide variation in the natural rates and rhythms of individuals in the class, class exercises to music should be used with discretion and not as the sole method of instruction.

As the child's skill grows, he may attempt more difficult exercises such as the following which, although appropriate to the primary stage, may nevertheless be found to be both enjoyable and profitable.

Running start

Linked letters ᘉᘉᘉᘉ ᓂᓂᓂᓂᓂ ᑐᑐᑐᑐᑐᑐᑐ

ᘉᘉᘉᘉ ᘉᘉᘉᘉ ᘉᘉᘉᘉ

(5) *Writing movements with pencil*

The emphasis in the exercises in the preceding sections has been on the rhythm and feel of the movement involved. Now, there must also be an increasing attention to improvement in the form of what is produced. In the exercises which follow, a more precise and restricted movement is demanded than formerly. It should be remembered that these exercises do not serve their purpose if the child is allowed to draw very slowly, carefully, heavily or jerkily. Each exercise should be repeated many times with increasing speed, rhythm and freedom of movement. The writing of letter forms should grow easily and naturally from these early free writing activities. It is always sound practice to associate the exercise with familiar objects or movements or to present it in the form of a story, e.g. swings, waves, fences, dress patterns, decorations for books or Christmas cards, toys, animals, etc.

Some of the exercises of this type are illustrated below.

The scheme of work and work books for infants contain many more examples. Many of the simpler shapes can be combined to make attractive patterns which will delight the child, especially if colour is used for part of the pattern or to fill in the spaces enclosed.

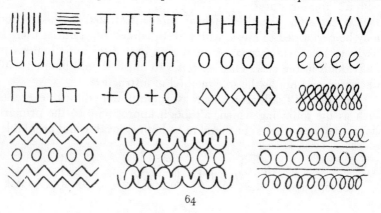

(6) *Writing letters, words and phrases*

Since handwriting is a mechanical skill, it must be based on sound mechanical principles. Exercises such as those described above and in the later stages, are necessary for the efficient and satisfactory development of the skill. Mere practice in writing, with occasional, casual instruction, just does not give the necessary amount or kind of practice required to achieve the high degree of skill needed to write speedily, legibly and gracefully.

Handwriting is also a means of expression and of communication. The child enters school with a fairly extensive vocabulary and will soon wish to be able to write words he knows and words he sees the teacher write. This desire must be stimulated and the child encouraged to attempt to copy words he has learned to read, to copy from his name-card and from labels on objects in the classroom. On occasion he will write a letter or word by the wrong series of movements but no great harm will result. The teacher will find many opportunities of showing how a letter or word should be written, but it must again be stressed that there should be no systematic, formal, letter by letter instruction at this stage. When the child attempts to write known words or even short meaningful phrases, the teacher's task should be to stimulate the desire to write, to encourage him to write freely and rhythmically letters of a size appropriate to his degree of neuromuscular development, to help him to acquire satisfactory writing techniques, and to guard against the emergence and growth of habits inimical to the full development of the skill at later stages.

2

Informal Instruction

There is no sharp distinction between the preparatory and infant stages. The nature of the instruction changes slowly in keeping with the developing abilities and needs of the children.

Many of the types of exercises suggested for the preparatory period continue to be used throughout the infant and even well into the primary stage. As the child matures he will be expected to perform them with ever increasing fluency and excellence of form.

Formal instruction in the correct method of writing letters is necessary if the child's skill is to be fully developed, but such instruction must be delayed until the child is able to read even to a limited extent and has had practice in writing the words and meaningful phrases he has learned to read. Even when formal work is begun, practice in writing and most of the instruction given, must continue to be through the writing of material which is of interest to the child because of its meaning.

Since individual children will reach the stage of readiness for particular forms of instruction at different times, the teacher will probably find it advisable to group the children for instructional purposes.

The nature of the instruction to be attempted during the remainder of the first year in the infant room is summarised below.

(1) Attention to the mechanics of writing.

(2) Exercises to develop neuromuscular co-ordination, and fluency, rhythm and quality of writing.

(3) The writing of meaningful words, phrases and sentences associated with reading and other activities. Incidental instruction

is given during this work, as the need arises, on the correct method of writing small letters, capitals and numerals. The methods described in Part One for teaching letters should be used. Emphasis must still be placed mainly on the fluency and rhythm of writing but a gradual improvement in quality must be demanded.

The schemes of work contain suggestions for writing activities of an informal kind, but a detailed scheme for this aspect of the work is not possible.

(4) Systematic instruction in the correct method of writing all small letters, capitals and numerals. Such instruction should start as soon as children become ready for it. By the end of the two years in the infant room the majority of children will be expected to be able to write all letters speedily and of good form even with the eyes closed.

(5) The work books, of necessity, deal almost exclusively with the work to be attempted during the periods of formal instruction. They also illustrate the pattern and rhythmic exercises which pupils may attempt.

FUNCTIONAL AND CREATIVE WRITING

As has already been stressed, the method of instruction in the early stages is to arouse the interest of the children through the functional and creative aspects of handwriting thus bringing them to recognise its value and stimulating them to apply themselves to acquire skill and proficiency in it.

To this end pupils first learn to write whole words within their vocabulary and understanding which they have met in their reading lessons, have seen on labels in the classroom or have seen written by the teacher on the blackboard, on cards or on their writing books. They see the teacher write, try to copy her and receive help from her when they do so. They also very quickly come to write short meaningful phrases or sentences allied to illustration.

The children will first watch the teacher as she draws a picture or pattern on the blackboard or demonstration sheet and writes freely underneath an appropriate descriptive phrase. Each child then makes his own drawings and description of the topic in free, vigorous lettering. In due course they come to make their own drawings or paste a cut-out picture on the page and write a descriptive sentence of their own. Each child will have a writing book of his own in which he writes his own short notes, descriptions and stories on topics of interest.

In general, writing lessons should arise as naturally as possible from a story or happening in the classroom and from topics suggested by the children themselves. The keeping of a class news sheet, calendars, weather and nature notes, class lists, milk, meals and attendance records, will also provide writing activities at this stage.

While the children are writing the teacher will find many opportunities for giving help and instruction to individual pupils. As occasion demands, she will also give lessons to the class or a group of children on the correct method of writing letters, the relative size of letters, the spacing of words and letters or the basic writing techniques. It must again be stressed, however, that the emphasis at this stage is mainly on the freedom and fluency of writing. The temptation to permit slow and laboured efforts to produce accurate letters and achieve a standard appropriate to a later stage must be resisted.

Soon the more able children will make demands on the teacher for ideas and material for writing practice. Cards written by the teacher may at first meet this need but it will be found that the work books contain very many examples of pattern and rhythm exercises, drawings, letters, words and phrases which will interest the child and give unlimited scope for individual and group practice of the appropriate kind.

Suggestions are given below of the detailed procedure which might be adopted in teaching lessons at two different stages.

Introductory exercises

(1) Relaxation exercise—right elbow on desk, hand in air, fingers loose, rotate the limp hand from the wrist in an anticlockwise direction.

(2) While the class watches, the teacher demonstrates on the blackboard or demonstration sheet how to write quickly and easily continuous anticlockwise spirals progressing from left to right.

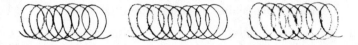

(3) The children practise this continuous anticlockwise movement in the air. When the teacher is satisfied that the desired movements come freely, the children are asked to write quickly across the top of their pages, a series of these spirals.

Learning to write a familiar word, e.g. dog

(1) The word to be written will already have been talked about because of its connection with some current reading or class interest and activity. The children will watch as the teacher writes the word on the blackboard under the pattern already drawn. The word must be written fluently and freely in reasonably large letters by the correct series of movements. As the teacher writes she may wish to give a running commentary on how each letter is written. The pupils say the word which has been written.

(2) The children are now asked to write the word in the same way under the pattern on their boards or pages. The teacher observes as they do so, gives help where required, and notes pupils who have difficulty with the mechanics of writing.

    The word written by each pupil must be looked at and

encouragement and advice given where necessary. Successful efforts should be praised.

(3) The less able pupils should have individual help from the teacher and further practice in writing the word. The others should have the opportunity of writing from cards words of similar form such as the following : go, do, good, fog, dad.

LESSON TWO

(1) A story suggested by the children or a brief description of an interesting happening is chosen after discussion.

(2) The words selected for writing, e.g. May we see John's rabbit? are written on the blackboard by the teacher. The children watch as she does so.

(3) The words used, the method of construction of words and letters, the relative size of letters and the spacing of the words may be discussed at this stage, and the children given an opportunity to practise difficult letters or words on their boards or sheets of paper, e.g. eee, John.

(4) Relaxation exercise.

(5) The teacher again demonstrates how the words are to be written freely and fluently, and after advice regarding the placing of the sentence on the page the children are asked to write it. As they do so the teacher observes them at work and gives advice and help as required.

(6) When they have finished, they are asked to read what has been written.

(7) While the teacher is helping children who have not succeeded in producing satisfactory work, the remainder of the class try to write their own story and illustrations.

A lesson of this type may start with a picture. The sentence is then written alongside.

Materials

The writing materials used in the infant room have been described on page 34, and the teacher is reminded of the following points :

Blank paper should be used. The teacher may find it helpful in the early stages to make a fold across the middle of the writing sheet or to divided the page into two or three by ruling a line or lines across the width of the page. The child then writes within the area marked —not upon a line.

Loose sheets of cheap paper should be used for scribbling exercises and preparatory work. Writing books, used for work which is to be retained, should have few pages. The earliest books should have pages measuring about 35×25 cm, but books may become progressively smaller as the child's skill increases.

3

First Year: Formal Instruction

INTRODUCTION

The general principles and methods on which formal instruction should be based are discussed in Part I. Details of method and suggestions for daily lessons are given in the schemes which follow.

Nature and Scope of Instruction

(1) Instruction and intensive practice in writing all small letters, capitals and numerals and commonly used words with attention to both the rhythm and quality of the writing. The aim is to endeavour to enable the child to acquire as early as possible firmly established motor habits for writing speedily, rhythmically and correctly all letters and many common words. Formal instruction and practice in writing capital letters is dealt with in the scheme for the second year.

    During the first year, incidental help and instruction in the method of writing capitals is given as the need to use them arises.

(2) Instruction and practice in writing whole words, phrases and sentences speedily and rhythmically with attention to the spacing of letters, words and lines and to the regularity and linearity of the writing.

(3) Pattern and rhythm exercises to develop the fluency of writing and skill in making handwriting movements.

(4) Constant instruction and help with the mechanics of handwriting to enable the child to acquire satisfactory writing techniques as firmly established habits at an early age.

Motivation

Children learn most readily when they are engaged on tasks which are obviously meaningful and purposive. Since the object of much of the work during these periods may not be immediately obvious to the child, it must be the constant concern of the teacher to make plain the purpose of the exercises. The child will take delight in acquiring skill in formal exercises especially if he sees how they can help his performance in class writing, if he is expected to apply his newly acquired skill and knowledge to such writing and if he can compare his skill and progress with his classmates.

A formal lesson might well start with the writing of familiar words which contain the letter to be practised. The lesson will usually finish with the writing of similar words or sentences during which the pupil will be expected to put his new knowledge or skill to use.

Scheme of Work and Work Books

The scheme of work has been arranged as a series of daily lessons. These lessons are arranged in groups, each group dealing with a particular aspect of the instruction, such as the method of writing letters of similar construction. For the first lesson in each group, the teaching procedure to be followed and the ancillary exercises to be used are explained in some detail : the remaining lessons in the group are given in outline.

The scheme contains a page by page reference to the Work Books in which are illustrated the prototypes of letters and words to be written in each lesson, the rhythmic pattern or drawing exercises associated with the lesson, the spacing of letters, words and lines appropriate to each stage, the relative size of letters and the setting out of material.

The teacher is not expected to adhere rigidly either to the order or content of the lessons set out in the scheme. A lesson which arises naturally out of some activity or point of interest in the classroom is usually to be preferred, but this is not always possible and at times it may not be desirable to interrupt the continuity of instruction. The scheme of lessons is intended to provide a systematic and comprehensive guide as to what may be attempted at any particular stage of instruction.

Surprise may be expressed regarding the order in which groups of letters are dealt with in the scheme, and it may be considered that it would have been logical to start with letters of simple construction such as *i*, *l* and *t*. The scheme has been so constructed that the teacher can start with this or any other group if she desires to do so.

It should be borne in mind, however, that the child is not writing for the first time but will already have had a fair amount of practice in writing most, if not all of the letters in the alphabet. He has been writing and will continue to write words in which vowels occur more frequently than any other letters, and there is, therefore, a case for teaching these letters at an early stage. There is also some evidence to show that children are in the earliest stages able to write oval letters such as *o* and *a* more easily than straight stroke letters, since the latter demand a higher degree of precision of limited movement and of judgement of relative size.

It will be found necessary to devote two or three lessons to teaching the more difficult letters, but a single lesson may be sufficient for some letters especially if the basic movement has already been learned. The teacher must determine, according to the progress made by the pupils, whether to increase or decrease the time suggested in the scheme for teaching a particular letter or group of letters. It will be understood that revision other than that allowed for in the scheme will be necessary. The work set out in the scheme for each year can be covered in about 30 weeks, so that the teacher will have time to undertake revision lessons if the need to do so becomes apparent.

The Small Letters

It is very important that adequate attention be paid in the early stages to the development of satisfactory writing techniques. Every time children write, the teacher must watch for those who adopt unsatisfactory postures, hold or use the writing instrument in an undesirable manner or are unable to write freely and rhythmically because of muscular or nervous tension. Only by constant instruction and help will the child be able to develop efficient writing habits and avoid the growth of those inimical to the full development of his skill.

Instruction and insistence on correct posture and pencil-hold must never be such that the child's desire to write or his pleasure in writing is diminished in any way. The diagrams of posture and pencil-hold shown in Part One illustrate the goal to be aimed at, rather than the standard to be achieved by the majority of children at the end of the infant stage.

Before formal instruction in writing letters begins, a few brief lessons ' How to Write ' should be given. Reference should be made to Part One, pages 15 to 19.

The following procedure can be used :

(1) Ensure that each child is provided with a seat and desk suited to his stature.

(2) Show the children how to sit correctly at the desk. A few simple rules such as the following may be memorised.

    (*a*) Feet flat on the floor
    (*b*) Body bent forward slightly
    (*c*) Head away from the paper and not turned to the side
    (*d*) Elbows off the desk
    (*e*) Hand and arms able to move easily

(3) Show the child how to hold a pencil in a reasonably correct manner. A drill such as the following has been found to be helpful.

75

(*a*) Lift pencil from the desk with the left hand.

(*b*) Hold right hand in writing position with muscles loose and forefinger slightly curved.

(*c*) Place pencil between the thumb and forefinger in the correct writing position and hold it very lightly with them about $2\frac{1}{2}$ cm from the point.

(*d*) Let middle finger rest lightly against the pencil.

(*e*) Hold pencil very lightly.   Do not press heavily on the paper when writing.

Formal rules such as those listed above are liable to induce undesirable tension if applied too strictly, but a few formal lessons followed by frequent reminders are necessary if correct and efficient writing techniques are to be established.

(4) While formal instruction on writing techniques is being given, children should not be asked to write letters and words.

The scribbling, pattern and drawing exercises illustrated in the Preparatory Scheme, pages 58 to 64 and on pages 1 to 5 of Work Book A, should be used to give practice in writing movements while the child is learning to hold the pencil in the way he has been shown.

(5) Teach the children several relaxation exercises which they can use for themselves at any time they write.   They should know why these exercises are used (see page 19).

RHYTHMIC SCRIBBLING EXERCISES   *Work Book A, page 1*

Exercises such as those illustrated on page 1 of Work Book A have a twofold purpose :

(1) to provide material for practice while instruction is given on correct posture and the correct method of holding and using a pencil

(2) to give practice in moving the pencil fluently and rhythmically.

The teacher can introduce the first exercise by drawing on the blackboard a simple chimney and showing how smoke from it can be represented by spiralling scribbles.

The children then perform the exercise over and over again on scrap sheets of paper. While they do so the teacher helps pupils who adopt unsatisfactory postures or who hold or use the pencil in an unsatisfactory manner. The aim is to make the movements as smoothly and rhythmically as possible. While great speed is unnecessary, slow, laboured writing should be discouraged.

The other exercises on page 1 are to be performed in the same manner and each can either be introduced by a demonstration on the blackboard by the teacher, or the more able children may be allowed to proceed to other exercises without further instruction.

There is no need for the children to draw a chimney, ball of wool, bird's nest or box of matches, though pupils who have completed an exercise satisfactorily may be usefully occupied in doing so.

Many similar types of exercises can be devised by the teacher and each should, if possible, be associated with a movement, e.g.

(*a*) Continuous up and down movement on the same line—bouncing a ball or movement of a yo-yo.

(*b*) Continuous up and down movement progressing across the page —bouncing a ball whilst walking.

(*c*) Continuous circular motion, clockwise and also anticlockwise— wheel turning, aeroplane propellor, windmill.

(*d*) Lines representing the path of a bird swooping, a frog jumping or a ball rolling, bounding and rebounding off the ground or a wall (see exercises at the top of pages 2, 3, 4, 5 and 6). The movement is to be made freely, smoothly and rhythmically with little attention to the appearance of the finished page.

RHYTHMIC DIRECTED MOVEMENTS   *Work Book A, pages 2 to 4*

The exercises illustrated on these three pages and on page 5 give practice in making the more precise and controlled movements which are the basis of all movements used in writing.

If possible, the teacher should associate each exercise with some form of movement. Each exercise should be practised many times until the child can perform it fluently, rhythmically and fairly accurately.

To aid the development of rhythm, the exercises can be performed to music, counting or nursery rhymes as described on page 61, Part Two.

Different movements can be combined as shown at the bottom of each page, to make patterns and give variety of practice. Practice may also be extended and made interesting by using different coloured pencils for each part of the pattern.

These basic handwriting movements and patterns made from them, are to be used frequently throughout the infant years. They are illustrated and used in various forms throughout the work books, and children are expected in time to be able to perform them rhythmically, speedily and accurately.

Anticlockwise Letters : o, c, a, d and g
Numerals : o, 6 and 9

The basic shape of the letters *o, c, a, d, g* and *q* is an ellipse made with a rhythmical, anticlockwise movement. Several lessons should be spent in teaching the letter *o* since it forms part of the other letters in the group. Only when it can be written reasonably fluently and correctly should the teacher proceed to the other letters.

The procedure for teaching the letter *o* has been given in some detail. Since similar methods should be used for the remaining letters and numerals in the group, only suggestions for appropriate exercises, words and sentences have been given in the teaching notes for these other letters.

The method of writing numerals should always be taught as the need arises in the daily work of the class. Formal instruction and much practice in writing these numerals fluently and correctly must, however, be given at some stage. Since o, 6 and 9 are written with an anticlockwise movement and should be taught by the same

78

methods as are advocated for the letters in this group, they can be included in this stage. Formal lessons and practice on these numerals should not, however, be given at this stage unless the children are already familiar with them and need to use them in their class work.

Capital letters should be used and taught as the need arises, but formal lessons and intensive practice should be delayed to a later stage.

PREPARATORY EXERCISES   *Work Book A, page 5*

Page 5 of the Work Book has illustrations of useful preliminary exercises.

(1) Continuous ovals. Starting at the one o'clock position, continuous ovals are made to rhythmical counting. Practice on loose sheets of paper should be given frequently until the oval can be made reasonably rhythmically and accurately.

(2) Single letters. Intersperse practice on continuous ovals and drawings involving ovals with rows of single letters made in one complete movement.

(3) Drawings. Simple figures and animals can be used to sustain interest and provide additional practice. The teacher can illustrate the construction of the figures step by step on the blackboard. Continuous ovals should be used for the initial efforts, but when the child can make single ellipses reasonably rhythmically and well, this form of practice should be used only occasionally.

A great variety of figures (such as those illustrated on page 65, and below) may be made in this way to give further practice and used to illustrate the children's books.

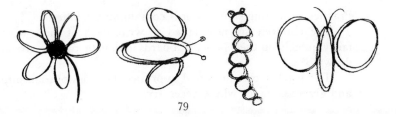

The method for teaching the letter and giving practice in writing it fluently and correctly.

Several lessons should be devoted to teaching this letter and in providing sufficient practice in writing it to enable the children to achieve a fair degree of skill in making it speedily, rhythmically and correctly.   Detailed suggestions as to the content of four lessons devoted to this letter are given below.

Lesson One

(1) Preliminary rhythmic exercise.

> The children watch the teacher as she draws freely and easily on the blackboard a series of continuous anticlockwise spirals.

(2) Relaxation exercise.

> After a brief relaxation exercise, the children draw quickly and easily similar patterns at the top of their pages.

(3) Simple words containing the letter *o*.

> The teacher mentions simple words known to the children which contain the letter *o* and then writes them freely and fairly quickly on the blackboard, giving a running commentary on the method of writing the letter *o* and any unfamiliar or difficult letters in the words.   (The teacher may find it advisable to deal with one word at a time but this will depend on the ability of the children in the class.)   e.g. so, go, no, good

(4) Practice in writing simple words containing the letter.

> The children are now asked to write each of those words fairly quickly on their paper or boards under the pattern already drawn.
>
> The teacher examines and appraises the work of each pupil and gives assistance where necessary.

Lesson Two

(1) The teacher refers to the previous lesson and explains that the object of this lesson is to learn to write the letter *o* quickly and correctly.

 She then follows the procedure explained in Part One, pages 10 to 14, summarised below, for teaching letters.

(2) Demonstration on the blackboard with a running commentary on how the letter *o* is written.

(3) Imitative movement—writing the letter in the air.

(4) Tracing the letter on the desk or over the large letter in the Work Book until the movement is correct and rhythmical.

(5) Writing the letter in groups of three with pencil on paper.

(6) Appraisal of the children's efforts by the teacher.

(7) Practice in writing the letter on scrap paper by children who have mastered the required movement. Children who have failed to do so should receive help from the teacher and may require to return to practise with tactile letters.

Lesson Three

(1) Relaxation exercise.

(2) Brief revision of method of writing the letter with emphasis on rhythm.

(3) Rhythm exercise. Continuous ellipses to counting.

(4) Continuous ovals followed by groups of three letters.

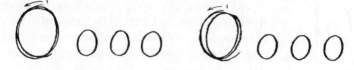

(5) Words containing the letter *o*, e.g. lot, hot, room, door, floor, our.

Lesson Four

(1) Revision and group work determined by the progress of individual children.

(2) Story-type exercise in writing book.
Picture or drawing of a dog and an appropriate sentence.
e.g. Does your dog beg for food ?
The dog begs for food.

(3) Pattern exercises such as those illustrated at the foot of page 6 of the Work Book.

THE LETTER *c*   *Work Book A, page 7*

 This letter should now present little difficulty, and two lessons will probably suffice. The teaching procedure should be as before.

(1) Relaxation exercise followed by rhythm exercise such as a row of continuous ovals.

(2) Words containing the letter, e.g. can, cot, ice.
Standard procedure for teaching a letter as in Lesson 2.

(3) Intensive practice in writing the letter fluently, speedily and correctly on scrap paper.

(4) Writing of words containing the letter and of appropriate sentence (allied to an illustration), e.g. cat, cool, cone.
Carol likes ice-cream cones.

THE LETTER *a* (Two or more lessons)   *Work Book A, page 7*

 This letter is to be written in a smooth, continuous movement without lifting the pencil from the paper.

(1) Relaxation exercise followed by a rhythmic writing exercise, e.g. continuous oval terminated by a single vertical downstroke resulting in the formation of the letter *a*.

82

(2) Words—am, at, cap, coat.

(3) Standard procedure for teaching a letter as detailed for the letter *o*, Lesson 2.

(4) Intensive practice in writing the letter. Rows of the letter *a* and of the letter alternated with the letters *o* and *c*.

(5) Sentence and illustration, e.g. Anne has a black cat.

THE LETTER *d* (Two or more lessons)   *Work Book A, page 8*

This letter is to be made in one smooth continuous movement as for the letter *a*. The oval part of the letter is desirably slightly more than half the height of the vertical stroke, but children may be advised that it is just half the height of the letter. The teacher need only be on guard against excessively large or small vertical strokes at this stage.

Exercises

(1) Continuous ovals terminated by an upstroke followed by a downstroke. Rows of alternate *d*'s and *o*'s

(2) do, did, doll, dog, daddy.

(3) Daddy has a dog. Dora's doll has a red dress.

THE LETTER *g*   *Work Book A, page 8*

This is another single stroke letter. The tail must not be too long or very curly. The teaching procedure is as for previous lessons.

Exercises (1) Continuous ovals terminated by a tail.

(2) go, good, egg, ago, dog.

(3) Peggy carries a basket of eggs.

This letter does not occur frequently, and when it does it is associated with the letter *u*.   It has, therefore, been associated with this letter in the Work Books and is dealt with at a later stage.

If, however, the teacher desires to teach this letter immediately after the letter *g*, the usual teaching procedures should be followed.

THE NUMERALS *o, 6 and 9*   *Work Book A, page 30*

Zero is made as for the letter *o*.   The loop of numeral 6 should not be closed.   The vertical stroke of 9 should not be too long (all numerals are the same size).

Revision of the letters o, c, a, d and g   *Work Book A, page 9*

When all the letters in a group have been covered, it will generally be advisable to spend a few lessons revising these letters with a view to improving (*a*) the form of the letters learned ;   (*b*) the speed of writing them ;   (*c*) the rhythm of writing.

Each letter should be written a great number of times, and page after page of scrap paper can be filled with rows of the same letter as the child strives to improve his performance.   The teacher must, however, keep a close watch on each child during such exercises to ensure undesirable letter forms are not practised.

Such practice can be followed by writing words and sentences which contain the letters in the group, e.g. go, good, dog, cod, coal, coat, cat, cool.

Page 9 of the Work Book contains some such examples of correctly drawn letters and words which can be used for revision work.

The Letters *q, u, e, s* and *f*

These letters, though they do not form a well-defined, closely related group, are placed together for convenience of instruction, and since anticlockwise movements are used in writing them.

PREPARATORY EXERCISES   *Work Book A, page 10*

Children should perform rhythmic pattern exercises such as those illustrated on page 10 of the Work Book before proceeding to the practice of letters in this unit.

Each exercise should be performed many times with a view to improving (*a*) the rhythm, (*b*) the quality, (*c*) the speed of performance.

The appropriate exercise should again be used as a preliminary to instruction in the writing of each letter in the unit. Combinations of the patterns can be used to form pattern exercises at the end of the lessons on each letter taught.

THE LETTER *q*   *Work Book A, page 11*

Little difficulty should be experienced in teaching this letter if the procedure detailed on page 81 for the teaching of the letter *o* and derived letters are used.

The termination should consist merely of a short upward flick as shown.

Rhythm exercises—continuous ovals with downward stroke and flick to produce the letter *q* :

(1) Pattern exercise—exercise 5 on page 10 of the Work Book.

(2) Use the standard procedure for teaching a letter as detailed in Lesson two, page 81.

(3) Words—up, cup, dug, hug, duck.

(4) Words using *qu*—queen, quick, quiet, queer.

This is a fairly difficult letter and several lessons may be required before it can be written rhythmically, speedily and correctly.

(1) Pattern—series of joined ' e's '.

(2) Words—me, we, he, she.

(3) Standard procedure for teaching the letter.

(4) Practice in writing rows of the letter and instruction of individual pupils by the teacher.

(5) Words—egg, deed, cage, see.

(6) Picture and sentence—The hen laid three eggs.

This is another difficult letter to write well, but preliminary practice with tactile letters will help the less able pupils.

(1) The standard procedure for teaching a letter should be used.

(2) Preliminary exercises—snakes and continuous figure eights.

(3) Words and sentence—so, see, sea, as, ass, does, dose, gas, sugar. This is the first class in the school.

Tell us a story please.

The top should be a simple curve similar to the start of the letter *s*. The cross-stroke is level with the top of small letters such as *o*. The letter is not quite so high as tall letters such as *l*, *h*, *d* and *k*, and should ideally be slightly taller than the letter *t*, but this latter distinction need not be stressed at this stage.

At the primary stage this letter is extended below the line and given a curved tail, but this form need not be taught to infants. The standard procedure for teaching the letter should again be used. No useful pattern exercises can be suggested for this letter, but as it is a difficult letter to write well at speed, additional practice in this aspect of the work should be given.

Words—of, off, snuff, puff, sofa, fall, face.

These letters should be revised with the aim of improving the form of the letters and the speed and rhythm of writing.

On page 14 of the Work Book, words and exercises are illustrated which can be used for revision. Such formal work can be done in the child's writing books after the intensive practice in writing on scrap paper has been satisfactorily concluded. Pupils may be allowed to illustrate words and sentences they write with appropriate drawings or pictures, e.g. goose, case, face, sea, desk, flask, fish, frog.

The Letters *l, i, t, j, and k*

These letters are not so easy to write well as might at first be assumed, as a fair degree of precision is demanded in their construction. The upright strokes must be vertical, the relative heights of the letters must be approximately correct at this stage and attention must be given to the spacing of letters when used in words.

Exercises such as those illustrated on page 15 of the Work Book not only provide useful preparation for writing the letters in this unit, but are invaluable at all stages of instruction for giving practice in making the precise and controlled movements required in writing.

(1) The continuous up and down movement illustrated in the exercise at the top of page 15 of the Work Book should at first be performed rhythmically to counting or to the repetition of a nursery rhyme. The downstrokes should be vertical, closely spaced and all of approximately the same height. Children should practise this exercise until they acquire a fair degree of competence.

(2) The second exercise on page 15 should be practised until the child can make the stroke correctly, speedily and rhythmically. The strokes should be vertical, all of the same height and equally spaced.

(3) The remaining exercises on page 15 add variety to further practice in making precise vertical and also horizontal strokes. A great number of exercises of this type, such as the following, can be devised by the teacher if additional practice is required.

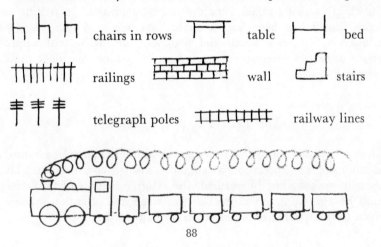

88

THE LETTER *l*   *Work Book A, page 16*

This letter should present little difficulty and there is
no need to follow the standard teaching procedure in
this case. Practice should, however, be continued
until the child can write the letter confidently, rhythmically and speedily.

The letter must be vertical. If a child writes with
a slant, the cause must be sought and a cure affected.
Pupils should not be allowed to write this letter by
flexing the fingers.

Tall letters should be almost, but not more than, twice the height
of the small letters. Pupils who fail at this stage to write letters of the
approximate correct relative height, should receive help and extra
practice in writing words containing letters of different heights, e.g.
log, leg, all, hall, doll, full.

THE LETTER *i*   *Work Book A, page 16*

A single lesson should suffice for this letter. It is the
same height as the other small letters, and the dot
should be placed at the correct distance, vertically
above the letter before the rest of the letters in the
word are written.

Words—ill, fill, hill, lid, lie, dig.

THE LETTER *t*   *Work Book A, page 17*

Two lessons may be found to be necessary for this letter.
The cross-stroke must be made horizontally at the
height of small letters and must cross through the
vertical stroke as illustrated. This letter is inter-
mediate in height between the small and the tall
letters. Practice should be continued until pupils
can make the letter of the correct height with the cross-
stroke made confidently and correctly.

(1) Patterns—vertical and horizontal strokes or telegraph poles.
(2) Words—lit, till, tell, little, hit, sit, sat, hot, letter.

2 The tail should not be too long or curly. It is made exactly as for the letter *g*. The letter should be dotted immediately it is written.

(1) Use the standard procedure for teaching the letter.
(2) Words—jug, job, jam, jump, jog.
(3) Sentence—John likes jam and jelly.

This letter presents some difficulty for children since it cannot be made in one continuous movement and judgment and precision is required in making the inclined strokes correctly.

Follow the normal teaching procedure for this letter, but after the demonstration on the blackboard of the method of construction, allow pupils to make the letter from three pieces of plasticine. When the pieces have been joined together correctly, the child should use the solid model as a tactile letter.

(1) Patterns.
(2) Words—like, cake, king, ink, sink, thank.
(3) Sentence—Thank you for the cake.

REVISION OF THE LETTERS *l, i, t, j and k*   *Work Book A, page 19*

These letters should now be revised with the aim of securing improvement in form and in the development of the speed and rhythm.

The letters *g, j* and *q* can also be compared at this stage.

The letters and some words using these letters are illustrated on page 18 of the Work Book.

Other suitable words are : luck, lick, kick, tick, joke.

These numerals can either be taught at this stage or as the need arises. The methods used for teaching the letters should be employed and the pupils given intensive practice by writing rows of the letter.

No pattern exercises are required as the writing of the numbers themselves gives the most satisfactory form of practice. Loops on 4 and 7 should not be permitted.

The Letters b, p, n, m, h and r

Clockwise movements are used in making the letters in this group. The letters obviously form two distinct groups but are for convenience all placed in this unit.

PREPARATORY EXERCISES *Work Book A, page 20*

Exercises such as close and open spirals, continuous loops, continuous and single ovals made with clockwise movements, should be practised intensively before teaching the letters *b* and *p*.

Examples of such exercises are illustrated on the upper half of page 20 of the Work Book.

Exercises such as those illustrated on the lower half of page 20 are a suitable preparation for the writing of the letters *n, m, h* and *r*.

THE LETTER *b* *Work Book A, page 21*

At least two lessons will be required for this letter. Much preliminary practice should be given in making clockwise movements, such as continuous and single ellipses and spirals.

(1) The standard teaching procedure for a letter as detailed for the letter *o* should be used.

(2) The letter should be practised intensively until it can be written correctly, rhythmically and speedily

(3) Rhythm exercise—vertical stroke followed by continuous clockwise spirals. Followed by rows of single letters.

(4) Words and sentence—be, ball, bat, baby, big, bag, balloon, bubble.
Bobby can blow big soap bubbles.

THE LETTER *p*   *Work Book A, page 21*

Procedure as for the letter *b*.

(1) Words and sentence—pot, pat, pen, play, cap, cup, puppy, pipe.
Peter picked a pail of apples.

THE LETTER *n*   *Work Book A, page 22*

(1) Preliminary rhythm exercise—

mm mm mm

(2) Follow standard procedure for teaching the letter.

(3) Pattern exercises and pictures such as bridge illustrated in Work Book using the letter *n*.

(4) Words and sentence—no, on, nine, bone, pan, penny, funny.
Anne needs a new pencil.

THE LETTER *m*   *Work Book A, page 22*

(1) Procedure as for the letter *n*.
(2) Words and sentence—me, my, mine, man, men, mother.
Mummy mends my summer dress.

THE LETTER *h*   *Work Book A, page 23*

(1) Standard teaching procedure.
(2) Words and sentence—he, him, hem, the, them, then.
Harry mends his chair with a hammer.

THE LETTER *r*   *Work Book A, page 23*

(1) Standard teaching procedure.
(2) Words and sentence—run, are, her, read, road, fur, hurry.
Robert reads his book under a tree.

SUPPLEMENTARY LESSONS

(1) *Numerals involving clockwise movements*   *Work Book A, page 30*

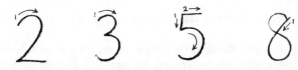

These numerals should be taught as required by the methods used for teaching letters. See Part I, page 45 for notes on numerals.

(2) *Revision of the letters b, p, m, n, h and r*   *Work Book A, pages 24 and 25*
Several lessons should be spent in revising the letters of this unit with the aim of improving the form of the letters and the speed and rhythm with which they are written. After intensive practice in writing the

letters and words containing them, pupils may make use of the formal lettering exercises on page 24 of the Work Book.

Words such as apple, bell, pram, plum, pear, orange, banana, grape, may be written in their exercise books and illustrated with a small drawing as shown on page 24.

It has been emphasised in Part I of this book that much of the instruction and practice in writing will be of an informal nature and that the formal exercises contained in the Work Books are merely a very necessary supplement to such work.

Throughout the infant classes, the children will frequently write their own little stories on topics of interest to them. On page 25 of the Work Book is set out such an exercise with illustrations. Although pupils may derive help from copying this page into their exercise books, its chief purposes are to show how a story and pictures can be set out on a page, to give guidance on alignment, spacing of letters, words and lines and also to give revision in writing the letters which have been taught in the preceding unit.

The teacher is expected to give frequently such exercises which may be based on happenings at school and on topics suggested by the children. When such an exercise is given, the teacher may find it helpful to refer children to pages 25 and 31 of the Work Book for guidance on the various points enumerated above.

Cross-stroke Letters v, w, x, y and z

These letters, though of relatively simple form, are not easy to make accurately, especially when written at speed. The child should practise writing these letters until he can write them speedily and well with his eyes closed.

PREPARATORY EXERCISES   *Work Book A, page 26*

Exercises such as those illustrated on page 26 of the Work Book should be practised before the letters in this group are taught.

The continuous movements involved in the first three exercises must be executed smoothly and rhythmically and may, with advantage, be performed to counting or music. Each exercise should be performed many times until the child can make the required movements confidently and accurately. A great variety of patterns, based on combinations of the elementary exercises at the top of the page may be made especially if coloured pencils are used. A whole page can be filled with each exercise or combination of exercises.

The more able children may be allowed to attempt the more difficult patterns and devise patterns for themselves while the teacher helps children who have difficulty in performing the simpler exercises.

THE LETTER *v*   *Work Book A, page 27*

This letter is to be made in a smooth continuous movement without lifting the pencil from the paper.

(1) Preliminary rhythmic exercise.
(2) Standard procedure for teaching a letter.
(3) Words—van, give, glove, have, vase.

THE LETTER *w*   *Work Book A, page 27*

This letter must be written without lifting the pencil from the paper.

(1) Follow standard procedure for teaching a letter.
(2) Words—we, were, was, wind, word, saw, wave, wigwams.

THE LETTER *x*   *Work Book A, page 28*

This letter is of course made with two separate strokes.

(1) Teaching procedure as for lessons 1 and 2.
(2) Words—box, fox, fix, six, mix, wax.

At this stage two strokes are used to make this letter. At the primary stage it is made in one continuous movement and has a curved tail.

(1) Teaching procedure as for lessons 1 and 2.

(2) Words—you, yes, my, very, many, your, yellow.

This letter is made without lifting the pencil from the paper.

(1) Use the standard procedure for teaching a letter.

(2) Words—zoo, zebra, lazy, buzz.

REVISION OF THE LETTERS *v, w, x, y and z*

The ability of children in the class to write these letters correctly and speedily should be tested. While the less able children are receiving further instruction and help, the more able members of the class may be engaged in pattern-making exercises and in writing words and sentences containing the letters.

Numerals ; Alignment and Spacing ; Revision

Work Book A contains illustrative material for the formal instruction to be attempted during the first year in the infant room, but it has been so designed that the teacher will still have time for very necessary revision.

This section contains suggestions for such revision and deals with those parts of the work which should be assessed and receive special attention.

It is expected that the numerals will have been taught during the year as the need to use them arose, and that they will have been taught by the methods recommended for teaching letters. They should, however, be practised intensively at some stage with a view to improving the form of the numerals and to developing the speed and rhythm with which they are written.

The numerals 1–10 and the method of constructing them are illustrated on page 30 of the Work Book.

If the children are asked to write one or two rows of each number on loose sheets of paper, the teacher will soon discover what remedial instruction and further practice by individual children are required.

Although the most efficacious form of practice is to write rows of the numerals which the child can write least well, this type of exercise should give way as soon as possible to the writing of meaningful material such as arithmetical sums already familiar to the pupils. These should be sufficiently simple to enable the child to concentrate on the writing rather than on the arithmetic involved. The excellence of the forms of the numerals, the fluency of the writing, the spacing of the figures and the layout of the sums are the aspects of the teaching which should be receiving attention from the teacher and child.

SPACING AND SETTING OUT OF MATERIAL

Work Book A, pages 31 and 32

The exercises on pages 31 and 32 of the Work Book may be used as the basis for a number of lessons, including guidance on the setting out of material, the size of letters, the spacing of letters, words and lines and the illustration of their written work. It must, however, be emphasised that there should be no attempt to force children to conform to standards at this stage. The freedom and rhythm with which the child writes and the delight he takes in writing are more important considerations at this stage.

Individual pupils will still vary widely in their ability to write, and they should be given considerable freedom to make letters of a size appropriate to their degree of maturation and to set out and illustrate their work to their own satisfaction. They must, however, be given guidance on the size of writing appropriate to a given exercise and to the size of the writing sheet used.

It will be found that the majority of the children in a class will all too readily tend to write as the teacher and classmates do, and to adopt the size of letters illustrated in the Work Books and on cards made by the teacher. The teacher will mainly be concerned with children who have not developed sufficiently to be able to write letters as small as those illustrated in the Work Books, and with those who attempt to copy adults and much older children by writing far smaller letters than is desirable at this stage.

The letters illustrated in the Work Books are of a size commonly written by the average pupil with pencil on paper at this stage, but as has already been emphasised, it would be wrong to expect all pupils in a class to write letters almost exactly of this size.

SPACING OF LETTERS AND WORDS

Guidance for the teacher on these aspects is given in Part One, page 43. The space between words obviously depends on the size of the letters used. For letters of the size used in the Work Book, the space between words should be such that the pencil can easily be placed between two words without touching any letter.

DISTANCE BETWEEN SUCCESSIVE LINES OF WRITING

There is no hard and fast rule, but in general, it is better to have too much rather than too little space between lines of writing. There certainly should be no likelihood of descenders in one line touching ascenders in the next. The spacing of lines in the Work Book gives a guide as to what might be expected at this stage.

ALIGNMENT AND PLACEMENT OF EXERCISE

Children must be taught to begin at the left-hand side of the page, to leave a space at the top of the page, to start a new line if there is insufficient room for the next word in a line, and to leave margins at sides and bottom of the page. The majority of the children in a class will soon learn these lessons and will be helped by using the Work Books, but there may be a few children in each class who will take longer to learn and will need continual help from the teacher until they overcome their difficulties.

A few children may have difficulty for some time in writing in a straight line across the page. Correction of faulty posture will generally quickly remedy this fault.

SPEED AND RHYTHM OF WRITING

It has been continually emphasised that the development of fluent and rhythmical writing is of more importance at this stage than the acquisition of the ability to write near perfect letter forms. Although the children should continually strive to write better letter forms and the teacher must always demand reasonably neat, tidy and careful work, it should be realised that children can readily improve the standard of their letter forms as they mature, if they have learned to write freely and rhythmically at this stage.

Slow, cramped, ultra careful writing performed in an attempt to acquire perfection of letter forms should never be permitted.

Exercises such as those on pages 31 and 32 of the Work Book should each be written several times. At the first attempt the passage may be written fairly slowly, but easily and rhythmically. It should be written several more times with care, but at gradually increasing speed on each occasion. Finally it can be written freely and easily in the children's exercise books and an appropriate illustration added.

If the teacher cares to test the speed at which individual children write (Part One, page 22), she will no doubt find much food for thought and readily discover which children in the class need further help and instruction.

4

Second Year: Formal Instruction

INTRODUCTION

During the second year in the infant room, the larger part of the practice in handwriting must continue to be through the writing of material which is of interest to the child because of its meaning. Incidental instruction in the mechanics of writing and in the correct method of writing letters will be given as required during informal writing periods and during writing in the service of other subjects.

Frequent but brief periods of systematic formal instruction must, however, continue to be given to consolidate and supplement such informal instruction, so that good writing techniques may be firmly established and the child learns to write letters and words rhythmically and correctly as unified motor habits.

Since the children in a class will differ widely in their knowledge and skill in writing, the teacher must first assess the level of ability and achievement of the children in the class, and base further instruction on their needs. Some of the children may require to continue to perform the exercises in Work Book A and receive instruction appropriate to an earlier stage than that reached by the majority of pupils in the class. It is therefore essential that the teacher be thoroughly familiar with the schemes of work and the methods of instruction employed in the earlier stages. She should also know how the work specified for her class is developed at later stages.

While it is natural for the teacher to seek a high standard of work from the children in her class, and while each child is expected to strive to improve the quality of his work, emphasis at this stage must continue to be placed on the freedom and fluency of writing by the child rather than on the attainment of an excellence of letter form appropriate to a later stage of instruction. The child's skill as a writer in later years will largely depend on the early establishment of sound writing techniques and on his ability to write fluently and rhythmically.

Very speedy writing is not looked for at this stage but fluent writing must always be encouraged. The slow and laboured copying of patterns, exercises, letters and words in order to attain copy-book form must be avoided.

Remedial Instruction and Revision

As has already been stated, the first task of the teacher must be to assess the ability and level of achievement of each child in the class and to adapt the instruction to the needs of each individual. It generally will be advisable to group the children for instructional purposes.

While the children are writing during an activity period, the teacher should attend to each child in turn, remembering that *how* the child writes is even more important than *what* he writes.

(1) See that the child is provided with a seat and desk suited to his height and build.

(2) Ensure that the child is seated correctly in a relaxed manner in such a way that the hands and arms are free to move easily across the desk (see page 15).

(3) Observe if the child holds his pencil in a reasonably correct manner (see page 16).

(4) Does the child hold the pencil lightly so that the teacher is able to pull it easily from between his fingers?

(5) Does the child write correctly by movements of the hand and arm or does he write by flexing the fingers?

(6) Does the child write fluently and rhythmically or is his writing slow, laboured and jerky?

(7) Has the child learned to write individual letters as a unified movement or is he still trying to draw a shape ?

(8) Have left-handed pupils acquired satisfactory writing techniques or do they require help and further instruction ?

(9) Examine what each child has written and check on the following:

  (*a*) Writing starting near the left-hand side of the page.
  (*b*) Alignment of writing across the page.
  (*c*) Spacing between letters, words and lines.
  (*d*) Lack of uniformity of size of letters.
  (*e*) Writing of a size suited to the child's degree of development.
  (*f*) Letters faulty in shape or proportion.
  (*g*) Pulled strokes should be vertical.
  (*h*) Parallelism of vertical strokes.

A procedure such as that described above will soon show the teacher what remedial work must be attempted and what aspects of the instruction must be revised with the class as a whole before new work is attempted. The next two sections are devoted to revision of certain parts of the work of the first year, but even before these are attempted, a check and remedial work such as described above will probably be advisable.

Rhythmic Pattern Exercises

The child will only be able to write reasonably quickly, freely and well when his neuromuscular co-ordination is sufficiently developed and he has acquired mechanically efficient methods of writing. The teacher's task is to foster the development of the child's skill by providing an almost unlimited number of writing exercises of an appropriate kind and to pay constant attention to the manner in which the child writes.

When the child is receiving remedial instruction on correct posture, relaxation and the correct method of holding and using a pencil, he should be given scribbling exercises such as those illustrated for the Preparatory Stage and at the beginning of Work Book A. The first four pages of Work Book B illustrate similar though slightly more difficult exercises for this purpose. These exercises incorporate all the movements used in the formation of letters and can be used for practice in making writing movements rhythmically to music or counting.

A learner's black pencil, coloured pencils, or an ordinary pencil with a holder are the appropriate writing instruments for these exercises. Each exercise should be performed over and over again, with the emphasis on the ease and rhythm of movement. Some of the patterns can be used to decorate cards and pages of the child's writing book, but even then the child should not be allowed to make slow laboured movements in the endeavour to achieve accuracy of form.

RHYTHMIC WRITING EXERCISES : OVALS   *Work Book B, page 1*

A few of the exercises which may be given to develop skill in making ovals are illustrated on this page. Rows of flowers, apples, rabbits, etc., should be made with the emphasis as always on the ease and rhythm of production rather than on the accurate representation of the form. Continuous ovals should be used for the earliest efforts.

The child should eventually be able to make a single oval reasonably accurately by a single, smooth, confident movement. Other exercises of this type are illustrated on pages 65 and 79, and on page 5 of Work Book A.

The clockwise and anticlockwise spirals, ovals and other movements illustrated on this page are to be practised until the child can perform them fluently and correctly. They may, with advantage, be performed on occasion to music or counting as described on page 61.

STRAIGHT LINE EXERCISES AND PATTERNS
Work Book B, pages 3 and 4

The exercises illustrated on these pages demand precision of movement and give the child appropriate practice to this end. Although at first they may be performed relatively slowly, the ultimate goal is the attainment of a confident, fluent and accurate movement. Other exercises of this type are illustrated throughout the Work Books, and the teacher should devise many more and use them very frequently throughout the whole course.

Revision of all Small Letters

The amount of time which should be spent on revision of the lower-case letters at this stage will depend on the degree of skill developed during the previous year by the children in the class. The teacher should assess the ability of each child to write each letter in the alphabet—

(1) by the correct series of movements ;
(2) speedily and rhythmically ;
(3) of an acceptable standard of accuracy and size.

This assessment will determine both the nature and duration of the revisionary work which is necessary. Some of the less able pupils may need to return to practice with Work Book A.

In general all pupils at this stage should have considerable initial practice in writing every letter correctly and speedily, followed by intensive practice with those which they write least satisfactorily.

The letters have been grouped in the Work Book according to the mode of construction. Appropriate rhythm exercises and words containing the letters are also illustrated.

THE ANTICLOCKWISE OVAL LETTERS *o, c, a, d, g and q*
Work Book B, page 5

(1) Preliminary rhythm exercises—anticlockwise spirals and continuous ovals.

(2) Brief revision of method of constructing each letter in the group followed by immediate practice in writing rows of the letter.

(3) Intensive practice in writing speedily, rhythmically and correctly each letter in the group.

(4) Words containing the letters of the group—cage, boat, dog, good, door, dot, goat, goal, gate, goose, coal, coat, school.

(5) Sentences containing many of the letters in the group.

THE STRAIGHT-LINE LETTERS *i, l, t, j and k Work Book B, page 5*

(1) Procedure as in lessons on oval letters.

(2) Words containing letters in the group—quick, jet, little, letter, tell, kick, tick, tilt, joke.

THE LETTERS *e, s, f, u, b and p* *Work Book B, page 6*

(1) Procedure as in lesson on oval letters.

(2) Words containing letters of the group—stuff, fluff, feast, first, feel, safe, soft, seeds, use, fuss, baby, butter, paper, papa, peep, pipe, bump, pump.

THE LETTERS *m, n, h and r* *Work Book B, page 7*

(1) Procedure as in lessons on oval letters.

(2) Words for practice—him, her, mine, nine, here, hear, hum, mum, man, many, then, them.

THE LETTERS *v, w, x, y and z* *Work Book B, page 7*

(1) Procedure as in lessons on oval letters.

(2) Words for practice—wave, wax, six, seven, next, lazy, zoo, zebra.

Capital Letters J, U, S, O, C, Q and G

The children will probably have had some instruction in the writing of capital letters during the first infant year as the need to use the letters arose.

The purpose of the next series of lessons is to consolidate such instruction and to give intensive practice in writing each capital letter speedily, rhythmically and correctly.

Pattern exercises are illustrated in the Work Books to give additional practice in making the required movements. Sentences and words using the capital letters being taught are also illustrated to lend variety and realism to the formal practice.

Reference should be made to pages 42 and 44 for details of the height, width and method of construction of capital letters.

CAPITAL LETTERS *U, S and J*   *Work Book B, page 8*

These three letters are used in the first lessons as they are the same shape as the corresponding small letters. During this series of lessons the capital letters and the corresponding small letter are illustrated side by side in the Work Books, so that the shape and the relative heights of the small and capital letters can be compared.

Children should be given intensive practice in writing individual letters, and words and sentences containing the capital letters, until they can write them confidently and well at a fairly reasonable speed.

Words and sentences for practice—James, Uncle John, Janet, Joe, January, June, July, September, Summer, Sunday, Saturday, Spring, Sally, Sarah, Sam, Ursula.

Sing a song of sixpence. Jack and Jill went up the hill.

CAPITAL LETTERS *O and C*   *Work Book B, page 9*

(1) Procedure as for *U, S and J*.

(2) Words and sentences—October, Olive, Owen, Oliver, Christmas, Charles, Clara, Colin, Cora.
    Cuckoo, Cuckoo, what do you do ?

(1) Since these capital letters differ from their corresponding lower-case letter, the correct method of constructing each letter will need to be explained. The methods for teaching the lower-case letters as detailed in the scheme for the first-year infants for the letter *o* on page 80 should be used.

(2) Compare the capital letter with the corresponding lower-case letter.

(3) Give intensive practice in writing the capital letter.

(4) Words and sentences containing the capital letters—Queen, George, Grace, Gillian, Goodnight, Good-bye.
God save our Gracious Queen.

Straight Stroke Capitals I, L, T, E, F and H

Although these letters are of relatively simple construction, a fair degree of skill and precision of movement is required before a child can write them speedily, confidently and accurately. Considerable practice to this end should therefore be given in making the pattern exercises illustrated and in writing the letters themselves. Words and sentences are given to add variety and realism to the practice.

PATTERN EXERCISES   *Work Book B, page 11*

A variety of such exercises are illustrated in the Work Books but the teachers should devise additional exercises suited to the needs of the individual child. The basic exercises consist of vertical strokes made by a movement of the pencil towards the body (made without flexure of the fingers). The strokes should be vertical, of uniform height or of the correct relative heights, and spaced uniformly :

Practice should continue until the child can make the required movements speedily, confidently and accurately. Rhythm of movement should be encouraged.

Similarly for horizontal strokes and combinations of horizontal and vertical strokes.

The teacher will be able to devise many such exercises as the following which the children can practice and use decoratively.

THE CAPITAL LETTERS *I, L and T*   *Work Book B, page 12*

(1) Teach the method of writing these letters by the correct sequence of strokes.

(2) Contrast shape and height with the corresponding small letters.

(3) Practice in writing these letters should continue until the child can write each letter confidently and correctly at speed.

(4) Practice words and sentences : Ian, London, Leeds, Lucy, Len, Tom, Tuesday, Thursday, Twinkle, Twinkle little star.
Tom, Tom, the piper's son.

THE CAPITAL LETTERS *E, F and H*   *Work Book B, page 13*

Procedure as for letters *I, L* and *T*.

Words and sentences for practice—Fred, Friday, February, Edward, Ena, Elsie, Easter, Harry, Helen.

REVISION OF *I, L, T, E, F and H*   *Work Book B, page 14*

The capital letters of this group should be revised by allowing children to write quickly a row of each letter in the group. Further practice should be devoted to letters which cause difficulty.

Additional practice with some of the letters in this group is provided by the exercise illustrated on page 14 of the Work Book.

The Capital Letters A, K, N and M

These letters can be constructed in various ways; the methods suggested on page 44 for doing so have been found to be satisfactory in the classroom. Other methods may be adopted if desired as long as a fixed method of construction is adhered to and the child given sufficient practice in that method. In general, the majority of movements should be pulled strokes.

LETTERS *A and K*   *Work Book B, page 15*

(1) Preparatory exercises.

(2) Contrast the form and height of the capital letter and correspond-ing small letter.

(3) Give the children instruction in the desired method of construct-ing the capital letter, followed by intensive practice in writing it.

(4) Give the children practice in writing and using the letter in words and sentences, e.g. April, August, Anne, Agnes, Arthur, Adam, King, Kate, Kenneth.

The Knave of Hearts stole the Queen's tarts.

Old King Cole was a merry old soul.

LETTERS *N and M*   *Work Book B, page 16*

(1) Proceed as for the letters *A* and *K*.

(2) Words for practice—Nora, Ned, Nell, Nancy, November, March, May, Monday, Mary, Margaret, Malcolm.

Mary, Mary, quite contrary.

Little Miss Muffet sat on a tuffet.

REVISION LESSONS

The capital letters in this group may be revised by allowing the children to write quickly and rhythmically rows of each letter in the group. Practice should thereafter be concentrated on the letters which are written slowly or of poor form.

Further practice in writing these and other capital letters is obtained from the exercise illustrated on page 17 of the Work Book.

Capital Letters *V, W, X, Y, and Z*

These letters, like those in the previous group, can be constructed by other methods than those suggested on page 44, but it is essential that pupils be taught and practised in one method only.

Pattern-making exercises can easily be devised to give preparatory practice for these letters. Examples for such exercises to be used both before and subsequent to practice in writing the letters are illustrated on pages 4 and 18 of the Work Book.

LETTERS *V and W*   *Work Book B, page 18*

(1) Preparatory exercises.
(2) Contrast form and relative heights of small and capital letters.
(3) Give instruction in the desired method of constructing the capital letter and then give the children intensive practice in writing it.
(4) Give the children practice in writing and using the letter in words and sentences, e.g. Violet, Vera, Victor, Wednesday, William, Walter, Wendy.

LETTERS *X, Y and Z*   *Work Book B, page 19*

Proceed as for the letters *V* and *W* then revise all letters in the group. Give further instruction and practice as required.

Capital Letters *P, R, D and B*

The correct proportions of these four capital letters and the methods of constructing them are illustrated on page 44. The vertical stroke should always be made first. These letters are illustrated in the Work Books with the curved part of the body starting at the vertical stroke, i.e.

P R D B

The letters should be taught in this way. When, however, the child is writing very quickly, it is difficult to ensure that the curve starts exactly at the line. It is then better for the curve to overhang very slightly than to stop short of the vertical.

The majority of children will require considerable practice before they can write these letters speedily, rhythmically and of reasonably correct form so at least two lessons should be allowed for each letter.

CAPITAL LETTER *P*   *Work Book B, page 20*

(1) Demonstrate on the blackboard the construction of the letter, with particular attention to the sequence and direction of strokes, the height and the width of the loop.

(2) Allow the children to trace the letter in the air, on their desks and with tactile letters if necessary. Follow this with practice in writing the letter on paper.

(3) Contrast the capital letter *P* with the small letter *p*.

(4) Give the children intensive practice in writing rows of the letter and words and sentences containing the letter. Give help and remedial instruction to individual children as required.
Peter, Polly, Pamela, Paul, Paris.
Polly put the kettle on.
Peter Piper picked a peck of pickled peppers.

CAPITAL LETTER *R*   *Work Book B, page 20*

(1) Proceed as for the letter *P*.

(2) Words and sentences—Robert, Ruth, Ronald.
Robin Redbreast sat on a tree.
Ride a cock horse.

(1) Proceed as for the letter *P*.
(2) Words and sentences—Bill, Bobby, Bert, Bunty.
    Little Bo-Peep.
    Little Boy Blue.
    Baa-Baa-Black Sheep.

CAPITAL LETTER *D*   *Work Book B, page 21*

(1) Proceed as for the letter *P*.
(2) Words and sentences—David, Dora, December, Dundee.
    Diddle, Diddle Dumpling.
    Ding Dong Bell.

REVISION OF CAPITAL LETTERS   *Work Book B, page 22*

Revise the capital letters in this group by allowing the children to write rows of each letter as quickly and rhythmically as they can. Practice should then be devoted to the letters with which the child finds some difficulty. At this stage all capital letters may be revised and remedial instruction given as is found necessary. Pupils should be given intensive practice in writing capital letters until each one can be written fluently and correctly. Practice may be diversified and made interesting by allowing the children to write notices using only capital letters, and by writing in capitals words to be seen in the school, e.g. HEADMASTER, STAFF, CLOAKROOM, JANITOR, FIRE, IN, OUT, ENTRANCE, EXIT, etc.; signs seen in the street, in shops and on traffic signs, e.g. STOP, HALT, GO, WAIT, SLOW, CROSS HERE, SCHOOL, HOSPITAL, etc. An exercise involving the writing of traffic signs may be illustrated as on page 22 of the Work Book.

Revision of the Lower-case Letters

A few lessons can profitably be devoted at this stage to revising the method of construction of the small letters and in giving further practice in writing these letters correctly at speed.

The teacher will be well acquainted with the standard of writing of each child in the class and will readily recognise what general revision and remedial instruction is necessary. Close scrutiny of the work of each child and of the manner in which he writes will, how-ever, show how much individual instruction is required. The ease, fluency and mechanical efficiency with which each child writes is still of more importance than the excellence of the letter forms he pro-duces. Although the next few lessons are concerned primarily with the size, shape and regularity of the letters and words to be written, the rhythm and fluency of production must not be neglected.

THE LOWER-CASE LETTERS   *Work Book B, page 23*
The alphabet is illustrated on page 23 of the Work Book. Children should be given plenty of practice in writing each letter many times, with a view to improving the fluency and standard of production. Individual children should be given remedial instruction and addi-tional practice with specific letters as is found necessary. Any tendency to write by flexing the fingers must be curbed immediately.

THE RELATIVE HEIGHTS OF LETTERS   *Work Book B, page 23*
The ascenders *b*, *d*, *h*, *k* and *l* should be almost twice the height of the small letters. This relationship is illustrated on page 23 of the Work Book. Practice with sheets of ruled writing paper for one lesson may help some children to appreciate the relative heights of letters but writing practice should thereafter be on blank paper.

Practice in writing letters of the correct relative heights can be obtained by writing a row of tall and short letters alternately and by writing words containing a mixture of tall and short letters, such as those illustrated on page 23 of the Work Book. All that should be demanded of the child at this stage is that the tall ascenders should all be roughly of the same size and about twice the size of the small letters when the letters are written rhythmically and fairly speedily. The pulled strokes of the letters are usually vertical at this stage. They must not slope backwards, but may be allowed to slope forward slightly if the child is able to write with such fluency and regularity that the strokes are parallel.

These two letters are the same height but are shorter than the tall ascenders. They are crossed horizontally level with the tops of small letters. The relative heights of these letters and types of words which may be used for practising them are illustrated on page 24 of the Work Book.

LETTERS WITH TAILS : *g, j, p, q and y*   *Work Book B, page 24*

The descending portion of these letters should be slightly less than the height of a small letter. This relationship is illustrated in the Work Book along with typical words for practice. The tails of *g* and *j* should not be allowed to become too long or curly and the letter *q* should merely be terminated by a short upward flick. The letter *y* has been used throughout the infant stage without a curl on the tail, but the form of this letter is changed in the schemes for older children.

RHYTHMICAL AND SPEEDY WRITING   *Work Book B, page 25*

During these exercises, there should be a deliberate striving to increase the speed and smoothness of specific writing movements. The endeavour must be to increase the speed and rhythm with which the exercise is performed, until the stage is reached at which further speed would result in loss of adequate control and unacceptable deterioration in the form of the pattern or letter which is being practised. For example in the following exercise illustrated on page 25 of the Work Book.

The continuous up and down strokes must be closely and evenly spaced and all should be of approximately the same size. The exercise can be done to counting or to saying ' down ' on each downstroke, and it should be repeated many times.

The other exercises on page 25 of the Work Book should be performed in the same way. It is most important that the child should not endeavour to acquire speed in these exercises by writing by flexure of the fingers.

SPEED OF WRITING   *Work Book B, page 25*

Speed by itself is of little importance at this or any other stage but both the teacher and children may find interest and value in measuring writing speeds. The method of doing so by writing the sentence, *Mary had a little lamb*, as often as possible in one minute is explained on page 22. The child who writes very slowly should not be pushed beyond his natural reactive rate nor forced to write quickly to keep up with his faster companions, for this can only result in the deterioration of his letter forms. He will only be able to write quickly and legibly when, through maturation and practice, his muscular co-ordination and ability to make rhythmical movements are sufficiently developed.

REGULARITY OF WRITING   *Work Book B, pages 26 and 27*

Good writing is always characterised by its regularity, that is the constancy of letter size and shape, slope, spacing of letters and lines, parallelism of downstrokes and the alignment of successive lines across the page. The teacher naturally has all these aspects of good writing in mind every time she examines and appraises a child's efforts, and indeed the danger is that greater importance will be placed at this stage on the appearance of the product than on the ease and fluency of production.

Some formal instruction must, however, be devoted to these aspects of good writing and the child should constantly strive to produce regular writing and neat and tidy work.

Two formal writing exercises are illustrated on pages 26 and 27 of the Work Book.

The teacher can make use of these pages to draw the attention of children to the spacing of words and lines, the relative size of letters, the use of margins and the placement of material on a page.

The children can be allowed to copy these passages into their exercise books and, although this may be done fairly slowly and carefully with the points which they have been taught in mind, they should also have the opportunity of writing the passages fairly quickly while striving to preserve the regularity of the writing.

LETTERS AND NOTICES   *Work Book B, page 28*

The majority of class writing exercises will be of interest to the child because of the meaning of the material and practical value of the exercise.   The child will frequently write little stories, notices and letters.   The teacher will be able to use the letter illustrated on page 28 of the Work Book to explain the layout of a letter or invitation, and the children can thereafter refer to this page when they are on later occasions required to perform similar exercises.   The children's exercises at this stage may well be enlivened by a coloured pattern at the top or the bottom of the page.

TOPICS   *Work Book B, page 29*

The page of words set out on page 29 of the Work Book has little value as such as a writing exercise, but it may well serve as the starting point for several writing topics or projects involving writing such as the making of a calendar.   The months may be dealt with separately and little illustrations and notes made regarding the weather, flowers or fruits associated with each month and season. Similar exercises associated with the days of the week, places of interest in the town, objects in the classroom, games, toys, shops, holidays and so on will suggest themselves to the teacher.

NUMBERS AND SUMS   *Work Book B, page 30*

The numerals will have been taught and practised as the children required to use them in their day-to-day work in class.   Page 30 of the Work Book is intended to serve as a source of reference during such earlier teaching, and to remind teachers at this stage that intensive practice is necessary if the numerals are to be written quickly yet correctly.

Although some of this practice will consist in writing rows of the numbers at increasing speed, instruction and practice will be given in setting down sums correctly with attention to the alignment of the rows and columns of the figures.

WRITING EXERCISES—*The Fruit Shop*   *Work Book B, page 31*

The teacher will be able to devise many writing exercises based on topics such as the 'Fruit Shop' illustrated in the Work Book. The Baker, Butcher, Greengrocer, Grocer, Ironmonger, Draper, Toyshop and so on will provide a source of words familiar to the children, and the teacher will find many opportunities for giving remedial instruction while the pupils are writing such words. The exercise can be made much more interesting if the children merely use the list of words illustrated to help them to write simple sentences about the shops and the goods they sell. Such exercises can be illustrated by little coloured drawings as in the Work Book.

PASSAGES FOR WRITING—*The Blackbirds*   *Work Book B, page 32*

The exercise illustrated on page 32 is typical of the kind of work the children can do in their writing books. The first verse of a poem they have been learning, a few lines of a nursery rhyme such as those illustrated on pages 26 and 27 of the Work Book, or a few connected sentences on a topic of interest can be discussed by the teacher with the children. Difficult words can be written on the teacher's blackboard and hints given on the placement on the page of both words and some form of illustration.

Although there will be a natural tendency to write exercises such as these slowly and carefully, the exercise should never degenerate into the meticulous copying of a page of the Work Book. The children's work should exhibit a liveliness and freedom of personal style which is understandably lacking in the Work Book letters. They should always have the opportunity of writing such an exercise with considerable fluency and freedom, preferably after it has been written with some care in their writing books. Both efforts should be of course examined by the teacher and praise, help and remedial instruction given.

If the formal work detailed in the schemes of work and in Work Book B is completed before the end of the school term, the teacher will readily recognise what parts of the instruction should be repeated and what revisionary practice is most necessary.

The mechanics of handwriting must receive constant attention. By the end of the second infant year, the majority of the children in the class are expected to be able to write all small letters, capitals and numerals fluently and correctly even with the eyes closed. They will only be able to do so if they have had a sufficiency of intensive practice in writing rhythmically and speedily. The size of writing, the relative size of letters, the correct form of the letters, the spacing of letters in words, the space between words and lines and the place-ment of writing on a page are all aspects of the work which may merit remedial-instruction and additional practice.

An important function of the teacher is to stimulate the children to take a pride in their writing and to strive to develop their skill and the quality of their efforts. When what the children write is to them obviously meaningful and useful ; when they feel that it is important to be able to write both fluently and well ; when they strive to improve their performance ; when they produce pleasing work which gives them satisfaction and they receive due praise for their efforts, then the writing lesson will be a joy to both teacher and child.